Aging in the Context of Urbanization

As China has undergone rapid urbanization and population aging in the past few decades, improving the welfare of older people in rural areas has become an ever more pressing issue. This is the first book-length work to examine the influence of urbanization on the mental health of China's older population outside the city.

Incorporating the theoretical framework of social ecology, the author analyzes the sociocultural factors that have exerted an impact on participants' mental health, such as their personal life course transition, changes to family living arrangements, and community restructuring. Moreover, he introduces several elderly mental health intervention models in China, while evaluating the policy initiatives that have developed based on China's local resource sufficiency, cultural customs, and older people's needs. The research findings not only facilitate a deeper understanding of China's welfare policymaking, but also offer a useful reference for countries that are experiencing similar urbanization and population aging and that wish to formulate better social policies.

Students and scholars of social policy, welfare, and gerontology will find this title to be essential reading.

Fan Yang is associate professor at the School of International and Public Affairs, China Institute for Urban Governance, Shanghai Jiao Tong University. His research interests are mainly social gerontology and social welfare policy.

China Perspectives

The China Perspectives series focuses on translating and publishing works by leading Chinese scholars, writing about both global topics and China-related themes. It covers humanities and social sciences, education, media and psychology, as well as many interdisciplinary themes.

This is the first time any of these books have been published in English for international readers. The series aims to put forward a Chinese perspective, give insights into cutting-edge academic thinking in China, and inspire researchers globally.

To submit proposals, please contact the Taylor & Francis Publisher for China Publishing Programme, Lian Sun (Lian.Sun@informa.com)

Titles in sociology currently include:

China's Middle Class
The New Social Stratum
Edited by Li Youmei

Northern and Southern China
Regional Differences in Rural Areas
Edited by He Xuefeng

Aging in the Context of Urbanization
Social Determinants for the Depression of the Chinese Older Population
Fan Yang

**Organizational Transformation and Order Reconstruction
in "Village-Turned-Community"**
WU Ying

For more information, please visit https://www.routledge.com/China-Perspectives/book-series/CPH

Aging in the Context of Urbanization

Social Determinants for the Depression of the Chinese Older Population

Fan Yang

LONDON AND NEW YORK

First published in English 2022
by Routledge
2 Park Square, Milton Park, Abingdon, Oxon OX14 4RN

and by Routledge
605 Third Avenue, New York, NY 10158

Routledge is an imprint of the Taylor & Francis Group, an informa business

© 2022 Fan Yang

English Version by permission of Shanghai Jiao Tong University Press.

British Library Cataloguing-in-Publication Data
A catalogue record for this book is available from the British Library

Library of Congress Cataloging-in-Publication Data
A catalog record has been requested for this book

ISBN: 978-1-032-16482-3 (hbk)
ISBN: 978-1-032-16485-4 (pbk)
ISBN: 978-1-003-24876-7 (ebk)

DOI: 10.4324/9781003248767

Typeset in Times New Roman
by Deanta Global Publishing Services, Chennai, India

Contents

Illustrations

Figure

Tables

1 Introduction

1.1 Population aging and urbanization in contemporary China

Population aging and urbanization will be the two fundamental demographic transformations in China in the next decades. The interweaving of the two profound transformations will not only shape the future development of the emerging economy in general, but also influence every individual in the country, especially older people's lives and bodily and mental health.

On the one hand, the Chinese population is aging rapidly. The fraction of the population aged 60 or over exceeded 10% for the first time in 1999 (National Bureau of Statistics of China, 2005), which is recognized as a symbol of becoming an aging society by the World Health Organization. In 2005, the 1% National Population Sample Survey showed that the older population reached 144 million, indicating China was the only country in the world with an older population of over 100 million (National Bureau of Statistics of China, 2005). The Sixth National Population Census of China in 2010 reported an older population of 178 million or 13.26% (National Bureau of Statistics of China, 2010), and according to the latest statistics, the Chinese older population had reached 254 million by the end of 2019, accounting for 18.1% of the total population (National Bureau of Statistics of China, 2020b). It is estimated that the Chinese older population will reach its peak by the middle of the 21st century, surpassing 400 million and occupying approximate one third of the Chinese total population (China National Committee on Aging, 2006).

It is worth noting that the rate of population aging is much higher in the rural than in the urban areas of China. While the share of the rural population keeps declining, from over 70% in the mid-1990s to less than 50% in the 2010s, the rural older population accounts for an increasingly higher percentage of the country's older population. According to the National

DOI: 10.4324/9781003248767-1

Bureau of Statistics of China (2010), 68.2% of the country's older people were in the rural sector, and the share of the older population was 11.7% and 15.0% in urban and rural China, respectively. With massive rural-to-urban migration of youth laborers, this disparity is expected to keep growing until 2040.

On the other hand, along with rapid population aging is another profound demographic transformation, namely urbanization, in China. Urbanization in modern China began between the late 1970s and early 1980s, when the country started the Reform and Opening Up policies (Chan, 2010). China saw steady urbanization progress between 1978 and 1995, when the share of its urban population had a yearly average increase of 0.64%; after that, China's urbanization accelerated and the share of its urban population had a yearly average increase of 1.39% between 1996 and 2012 (National Bureau of Statistics of China, 2012, 2013). Until the end of 2019, over 848 million people were residing in the urban areas of China, accounting for 60.57% of the total population (National Bureau of Statistics of China, 2020b). According to the National Plan for New Urbanization (2014–2020), the country will increase its urban population to over 80% by 2050, equivalent to the level of most developed countries (State Council of China, 2014).

This vast urbanization reflects the profound transition of China's social and economic system since the implementation of Reform and Opening Up in the late 1970s. It has also bolstered the country's economic miracle during the same period. In the process of transitioning from planned economy to market economy, hundreds of millions of Chinese rural people have migrated into the urban sector to pursue better jobs and other opportunities of climbing up the social ladder, as a result of the loosening *Hukou* (permanent household registration) system, establishment of the household contract responsibility system, and industrialization. According to the National Bureau of Statistics of China (2020a), more than 177 million rural people were working in urban areas until the end of the second quarter in 2020. It is not uncommon that in many rural areas nearly all youth laborers have migrated into urban areas while older people are left behind, which substantially weakens the role of the family in providing care for older people. According to the Fifth National Census conducted in 2010, China had 23.40 million older adults (65 years or above) living in empty-nest families, in which the children were not living close to the elderly. Among them, about 16.33 million were in rural areas, accounting for 69.79% of the total. This is a result of fast urbanization and is sharply different from the traditional family living arrangement that used to be prevalent in rural China, namely with three or more generations living under the same roof.

Therefore, the Chinese population is aging rapidly in the context of vast urbanization, and the trend will last until the middle of this century. This is in line with the world's general demographic transformations over the coming decades. Half of the world's population currently live in cities, and it has been estimated that this figure will surge to 60% by 2030 (Caiaffa et al., 2008; Quinn, 2008). At the same time, the world population of elderly persons may double from 11% to 22% by 2050 and will be concentrated in the urban areas of developing countries, representing 25% of the urban population of those countries (Quinn, 2008; World Health Organization, 2007). The effects of urbanization on population aging are multiple. Urbanization represents an expansion of urban space, the market, and the workforce, which will bring about changes at the individual, family, and community levels that may in turn become significant risk factors, as well as opportunities, for people's mental wellbeing from multiple aspects (Gong et al., 2012). However, previous studies focused more on the migrant population, while much less attention has been put on the impacts of urbanization on the mental wellbeing of the rural aging population (Zhang & Song, 2003; Zhang, 2008).

1.2 Urbanization and the mental health of Chinese rural older people

Urbanization may correlate with population aging through different pathways, and one of them is by affecting mental health of older people. Urbanization usually means the expansion of urban physical space, the market, and the size of the labor force, during which the changes occurring at the individual, family, and community levels could create positive or negative factors for older people's mental health (Gong et al., 2012). However, the existing literature mainly focuses on rural-to-urban migrants, such as the civil rights, the social security benefits, and the public health issues of migrant people. Little attention has been paid to the influence of urbanization on the mental health of older people living in rural areas (Zhang, 2008).

As a multidimensional social process, urbanization can influence human development outcomes from different levels. In other words, the social determinants of mental health in the context of urbanization shall be understood from an ecological perspective. In China's urbanization, various factors at the individual, household, and community levels can affect the mental wellbeing of the aging population. For instance, the individual-level pathway may include the transformations in social identity, physical health, and lifestyle; the household-level pathway may include the shifts in living arrangement, family relationship, and income; and the community-level pathway may include restructuring in social and physical infrastructure. All of these changes may have implications, positive or negative, on the mental health of the Chinese rural mature and older population.

1.2.1 Transformation of individual's social identity

As a type of institutional exclusion, the *Hukou* system first divides Chinese people into hierarchical layers and then organizes them into horizontally coexisting while separated subgroups (i.e., urban group and rural group) (Wang, 2005). Established in the 1950s, *Hukou* system was initially applied to control migration from the rural to the urban. This policy was sustained and strengthened in later decades through differentiating the allocation of various public resources (e.g., welfare benefits, education and health services, and favorable economic development policies) between the rural and the urban. Gradually, China forms a dualistic social structure, and people's social identity as a rural or an urban *Hukou* holder has sharply different implications with regard to citizenship rights. The urban *Hukou* holders, especially those in developed cities, have all-round priority in the country's social, economic, and political life.

For Chinese people, the *Hukou* identity is decided by the *Hukou* identity of parents and birthplace. Before the Reform and Opening Up in the late 1970s, the access to identity transformation was limited. The major ways of transforming rural identity to urban identity are two-fold, namely being accepted by a college or getting a decent job in the city. Due to disadvantages in basic education and technical training, the chances of successful transformation were quite slim before the Reform. With ongoing urbanization in the post-reform period, the rapid advance in the economy and in technology gave birth to huge excess labor in the rural areas while there were great labor demands in the urban areas. Also, wider access to information about the outside world encourages rural people to adventure into the urban areas. Therefore, China has seen tens of millions of rural people pouring into cities annually since the 1980s, eager to change their prescribed life course in the countryside. Most of the migrants get higher income in the urban areas, although their rural *Hukou* identity deprives them of access to welfare benefits and public services in cities. Meanwhile, some of them also manage to obtain the urban *Hukou* identity. Therefore, identity transformation or non-transformation is a useful angle from which to look into the effects of urbanization on individuals, mainly because it is a useful proxy for welfare benefits, lifestyle, and other social information for an individual in China.

1.2.2 Shift in household living arrangements

The living arrangements of Chinese rural families has been substantially changed in the process of urbanization. Traditionally, more than two generations living under the same roof or in proximity was prevalent in rural China. This has changed substantially since the late 20th century, when

China's urbanization accelerated. Between 2000 and 2010, the share of single-generation families in the countryside has increased from 18.21% to 29.77%; and the share of empty-nest families in rural families with older persons (65 or above) has increased from 20.98% to 29.60% (National Bureau of Statistics of China, 2005, 2010). Moreover, over 2.18 million households in rural China belonged to skipped-generation families by 2010, namely the family comprising older people and underage grandchildren (National Bureau of Statistics of China, 2010).

The major cause of the shift in household living arrangements in rural China is massive rural-to-urban migration. An overwhelming majority of the more than 200 hundred million rural migrants are of working age and do not have family members in the urban sector. This explains the increase in the share of single-generation families, empty-nest families, and skipped-generation families in the countryside. Special attention should be paid to the consequences of the shift in living arrangements of the rural aging population. The absence of adult children adds to their vulnerabilities in facing life stressors, such as loneliness and functional decline. For reasons of geographical distance, transportation expense, and work pressure, most rural migrants return home once a year or less (Wong, Fu, Li, & Song, 2007). Therefore, the rural elderly might receive quite limited support from migrated children in daily life. Moreover, many of them have to shoulder the responsibility of caring for the grandchildren left behind by the migrated children. Due to the weakness in China's rural public service systems, especially the education system, grandparenting can be another significant life stressor for the rural aging population.

Although consensus has been reached on the prominence of population migration in China's urbanization, more attention has been paid to the migrant population, mostly youth laborers, while the mature and older population left behind in the rural sector is relatively ignored (Zhang & Song, 2003; Zhang, 2008). For the affected rural aging population, living arrangements, especially the spatial distance from their children, can influence their mental wellbeing directly, or indirectly through family relationships, family support, and household income. As such, household living arrangements are the most significant factor influencing the mental wellbeing of mature and older adults in the context of urbanization.

1.2.3 Restructuring of the rural community environment

Chinese urbanization not only sees the concentration of various resources in cities but also the expansion of urban space and capital (Deng, Huang, Rozelle, & Uchida, 2008). With the deepening of urbanization, cities need more space to accommodate the increased population and industries, and the most straightforward measure to address the problem is to expropriate land from rural communities. Since the late 1980s, the country has recorded a continuing expropriation of rural land amounting to millions of *mu* each year (Guo, 2001). The area covered by China's urban regions increased by 74.6% between 2000 and 2011 (State Council of China, 2014). With more ambitious urbanization schemes being proposed and implemented, more rural land will be expropriated in the foreseeable future.

Land is at the core of social and economic life in the countryside, the loss of which means the most fundamental changes for rural communities. At the individual level, rural people have to change their occupation, namely from farming to positions in service industry or manufacturing, or just become unemployed. They may also experience changes in housing, lifestyle, income level, and many others. At the community level, the physical environment will be changed first. Since rural land is mostly expropriated for industrial and residential purpose, modern infrastructure (e.g., road, bus services, amenity facilities) will be established or upgraded in the affected communities. Further, the economic structure will also be changed, taking the form of agriculture receding and the establishment of more factories and commerce. The social environment in rural communities will also be transformed, namely from a traditional acquaintance society with blood linkage to a more plural society linked by mutual help and common hobbies and interests. However, previous studies have suffered from the methodological limitation of focusing on either physical factors or social environment factors. Considering the features of China's urbanization at the community level, there is a need to take both of them into consideration when investigating their mental health implications.

To sum up, various factors at the individual, household, and community levels can affect the mental wellbeing of the aging population in China's urbanization. The most significant factor at the individual level is the social identity shaped by the *Hukou* system; the most significant factor at the household level is the living-arrangement change resulting from massive rural-to-urban migration; and the most significant factor at the community level is community restructuring led by land expropriation in the rural areas. The mental health implications of urbanization in China will be examined from the points of view of social identity transformation, household living arrangement shifts, and community environment restructuring.

1.3 Research aims and significance

This book is aimed at investigating how the urbanization process influences the mental wellbeing of the Chinese rural older population. Specific attention will be given to the influences at the individual, household, and community levels of urbanization on the depression of Chinese older people living in rural communities. Moreover, policy initiatives that are implemented to protect the mental health of rural older populations will be discussed and compared. Therefore, the aims for this research are two-fold:

1. To investigate how individual life-course transition, family living-arrangement variation, and community environment restructuring resulting from urbanization are associated with the depression of the Chinese rural older population;
2. To generate policy implications by conducting case studies of the representative models of elderly mental health promotion, including ones that are localized from models developed in Western countries and ones developed in the local context of rural China.

This research has theoretical and empirical significance. Theoretically, it contributes to enriching our understanding of the different levels of social determinants for mental health, namely individual life course, household living arrangements, and community environment restructuring. First, it streamlines the association between early-life experience (i.e., childhood adversity) and depressive symptoms in later life. Existing literature has ambivalent findings on whether adverse experience in early life is associated with mental health in later life (Black & Ford-Gilboe, 2004; Green et al., 2010; Wainwright & Surtees, 2002), and little research has been found on investigating how things that happened in between the early life and later life stages moderate/mediate the association. Current Chinese rural mature and older populations have experience urbanization in their adulthood. Therefore, by making individual urbanization experience a moderator, this research provides a useful method to streamline the correlation between early life experience and human development outcome in later life.

Second, this research adds to the understanding of the implications of family spatial separation on the mental health of the aging population. The existing literature mainly delves into the influence of spatial separation from family members on elderly mental health through the perspective of resources (Hank, 2007). In the context of China's urbanization, it means that the out-migration of children may affect instrumental support resources, monetary and in-kind support resources, and emotional support resources for the older people left behind (Guo, Aranda, & Silverstein, 2009). However, due to the distinctions in the causes of family separation, family structure, and the economic and cultural traits of the aging population, spatial separation between family members may influence the aging population differently through the pathway of family resources in a developing country like China. Therefore, a multidimensional perspective will be applied to examining the mental health implications of family spatial separation for the Chinese rural aging population.

Third, this research extends the understanding of the mental health implications of community restructuring. A large volume of literature has demonstrated that an individual's mental health is closely associated with the community environment (e.g., availability of infrastructure, amenities, and grassroots organization) he/she is attached to (Halpern, 2014). However, while some studies have reported that community restructuring is associated with negative influences on mental health through bringing in stressful lifestyles, polluted environments, and inadaptability to change (Chen, Chen, & Landry, 2013; Harpham & Molyneux, 2001), some other research reveals that through expanding access to employment, education, and other opportunities for upward social mobility, community restructuring may confer positive effects on the mental health of community-based adults (Fraser et al., 2005). Therefore, by investigating the mental health effects of physical and socioeconomic environment changes in the rural community, this study contributes to theories of community environment and mental health in later life.

Moreover, this research has empirical significance in shaping urbanization policies that cater for the mental health needs of the Chinese rural and mature population. China's urbanization policies in the past decades have been instrumentalism-based, focusing on economic development while largely ignoring the psychological wellbeing of people in the affected areas. For instance, the goal of GDP growth and basic infrastructure constructions, such as building roads, bridges, squares, and high-rise towers, have been prioritized in past urbanization policies. This style of urbanization has been criticized as "land urbanization" rather than "people urbanization" (Chen, Zhang, Wu, & Zhang, 2010). The resulting social inequalities and exclusion can be especially challenging for the rural older population, considering their disadvantages in coping with and adapting to social transformation (Abbott & Sapsford, 2005).

According to the National Plan for New Urbanization (2014–2020) issued by the National Committee on Development and Reform in 2014, China will implement a people-centered urbanization. To reach the goal, more policy emphasis should be placed on vulnerable populations (e.g., the older population) whose development and interests are affected in urbanization. At the same time, it is also worth noting that the current urbanization process could be a rare opportunity to shape an equal, inclusive, and empowering urban environment for a rapidly enlarging older population. Analysis of the role of social identity, living arrangements, and community environment restructuring can shed light on policy implications in this respect. Moreover, China's experience and lessons in developing intervention models and programs of human services in the context of social transformation provide a desirable angle to look into the functioning of Chinese society.

1.4 Research methods and structure of the book

This research is based on a mixed method approach, combining both quantitative and qualitative data collected in China. In exploring the individual-, family-, and community-level influencing factors of rural older people's depression in the context of urbanization, secondary quantitative data analysis will be utilized; in examining China's localization of foreign countries' models, as well as China's local initiatives, on elderly mental health, case studies will be applied; moreover, theories and empirical evidence on elderly mental health and its influencing factors will be systematically reviewed. Statistical analysis methods, such as descriptive statistics, regression analysis, latent class analysis, and multilevel analysis, will be applied to analyzing quantitative data. For instance, multilevel analysis will be used to reveal the influence of community-level factors on Chinese rural older people's depression; and latent class analysis will be utilized to investigate the clusters among different childhood adversities and how they are associated with life-course transitions and depression in later life. Statistical analyses will mainly use SPSS 23.0 and Mplus 8.0. Moreover, comparative case studies will be applied to describe how elderly mental health promotion and/or intervention models are implemented in China, as well as how they are different from similar programs in Western countries.

The first chapter of the book is an introduction to the key research concepts. It mainly discusses three concepts, namely urbanization, population aging, and elderly depression, as well as how the three may associate with each other according to past literature. The discussion will incorporate global findings and further raise the core research question of the present book: that is, how does the urbanization process influence the depression of the Chinese rural older population? The theoretical and empirical implications of answering this question in contemporary China will also be discussed.

Chapter 2 discusses the associations between urbanization and mental health of the Chinese rural older population from three aspects. Firstly, it reflects on the history of China's urbanization since 1949 when the People's Republic of China was founded. Based on a comparison with the world's urbanization history, it performs a topological analysis on China's urbanization in different historical periods. This facilitates a clearer identification of the characteristics and influencing factors of contemporary China's urbanization. Secondly, it systematically summarizes the potential social determinants of depression/mental health of the older population, especially those relating to life course, family relations, and community development. This paves the way for the analysis of the influencing factors for the depression of the Chinese rural older population in the later parts of the book. Thirdly, it presents a general picture of the incidence and prevalence of various mental health problems among Chinese rural older people, based on statistics from the major national representative datasets. The potential social determinants will be discussed, and the emphasis will be on the negative effects of mental health problems, especially depression, on the bodily health, disability, behavioral health, and social and family relations of Chinese rural older people.

Chapter 3 introduces the theoretical framework and data sources used in this book. This research is based on the social ecology perspective, which is used to understand how urbanization influences the depression of rural older people in China. At the same time, this chapter conceptualizes these influences into three layers, namely life-course transition at the individual level, family living-arrangement change at the household level, and environmental restructuring at the community level. Specifically, the developmental adaptation model (DAM) is used in the individual-level analysis; the stress-buffering model is used in the household-level analysis; and the fundamental causes theory is applied in analyzing the community-level effects of urbanization on the depression of the older population. This chapter also introduces competing theories and explains why they are not the most appropriate ones in this research. Moreover, the secondary datasets used in the quantitative part of the book, namely China Health and Retirement Longitudinal Study (CHARLS), and the cases and intervention models analyzed in the qualitative part of the book will be briefed in this chapter.

Chapter 4 reports the quantitative findings of the research. It disentangles the influences of urbanization on the depression of the Chinese rural older population from three aspects, namely social identity transition in the individual life course, family living arrangement variations, and community environment restructuring.

Chapter 5 is mainly on the localization of popular care models in Western countries in urbanizing China. Specific attention will be paid to the Program of All-Inclusive Care for the Elderly (PACE), the time bank solution, and the gatekeeper training for suicide prevention, as well as their local versions in urbanizing China. Though these programs are not specifically for depression intervention, they have been widely used to improve the general mental health of community-dwelling older people. Moreover, they are receiving increased policy attention in the fast urbanization of China, and thus are often embodied in local governments' community-building strategies. In this part, three cases in urbanizing China will be discussed, including the Comprehensive Services Center for the Elderly (综合为老服务中心), Time Bank, and the Mental Health Crisis Intervention Program for the Rural Elderly.

Chapter 6 focuses on China's locally developed initiatives on elderly mental health promotion. Apart from drawing on foreign experience, many Chinese communities have developed intervention models that cater to local resource sufficiency, cultural customs, and older people's needs. In this part, the mutual-support care model and the dementia-friendly community model will be discussed. The two models are developed mainly to deal with the weakening role of family in supporting rural elderly people in urbanization. That is, the rural youth population migrates to the urban sector to pursue better job opportunities, leaving their elderly family members behind, which not only deprives the rural older people of daily instrumental support from the younger generation, but also leads to negative mental health consequences.

Chapter 7 is a summary of the whole book. It disentangles the core principle of China's urbanization policies, namely person-centeredness, as well as its emphasis on the mental health of the affected older people through the perspective of affection-based governance. Then, it acknowledges the research limitations and proposes policy suggestions according to the research findings. In particular, these findings might have policy implications for developing countries that are undergoing fast urbanization and population aging. At the same time, it discusses the directions for future studies to consider when researching into the associations between urbanization and population aging.

References

Abbott, P., & Sapsford, R. (2005). Living on the margins: Older people, place and social exclusion. *Policy Studies, 26*(1), 29–46. doi:10.1080/01442870500041660.

Black, C., & Ford-Gilboe, M. (2004). Adolescent mothers: resilience, family health work and health-promoting practices. *Journal of Advanced Nursing, 48*(4), 351–360. doi:10.1111/j.1365-2648.2004.03204.x

Caiaffa, W. T., Ferreira, F. R., Ferreira, A. D., Oliveira, C. D. L., Camargos, V. P., & Proietti, F. A. (2008). Urban health:" The city is a strange lady, smiling today, devouring you tomorrow". *Ciencia & Saude Coletiva, 13*(6), 1785.

Chan, K. W. (2010). Fundamentals of China's urbanization and policy. *China Review, 10*(1), 63–94.

Chen, F., Zhang, H. o., Wu, Q., & Zhang, W. (2010). Research on the coordination of China's population urbanization and land urbanization (in Chinese). *Human Geography, 5*, 53–58.

Chen, J., Chen, S., & Landry, P. F. (2013). Migration, environmental hazards, and health outcomes in China. *Social Science & Medicine, 80,* 85–95.

China National Committee on Aging. (2006). Research report on the trend of China's population aging. Retrieved from http://www.ctc-health.org.cn/file/20061213 lnqs.pdf

Deng, X., Huang, J., Rozelle, S., & Uchida, E. (2008). Growth, population and industrialization, and urban land expansion of China. *Journal of Urban Economics, 63*(1), 96–115. doi:10.1016/j.jue.2006.12.006

Fraser, C., Jackson, H., Judd, F., Komiti, A., Robins, G., Murray, G., … Hodgins, G. (2005). Changing places: The impact of rural restructuring on mental health in Australia. *Health & Place, 11*(2), 157–171.

Gong, P., Liang, S., Carlton, E. J., Jiang, Q., Wu, J., Wang, L., & Remais, J. V. (2012). Urbanisation and health in China. *The Lancet, 379*(9818), 843–852. doi:10.1016/S0140-6736(11)61878-3

Green, J. G., McLaughlin, K. A., Berglund, P. A., Gruber, M. J., Sampson, N. A., Zaslavsky, A. M., & Kessler, R. C. (2010). Childhood adversities and adult psychiatric disorders in the national comorbidity survey replication I: Associations with first onset of DSM-IV disorders. *Archives of General Psychiatry, 67*(2), 113–123. doi:10.1001/archgenpsychiatry.2009.186

Guo, M., Aranda, M. P., & Silverstein, M. (2009). The impact of out-migration on the inter-generational support and psychological wellbeing of older adults in rural China. *Aging and Society, 29*(7), 1085.

Guo, X. (2001). Land expropriation and rural conflicts in China. *The China Quarterly, 166,* 422–439.

Halpern, D. (2014). *Mental Health and the Built Environment: More Than Bricks and Mortar?.* London: Routledge.

Hank, K. (2007). Proximity and contacts between older parents and their children: A European comparison. *Journal of Marriage and Family, 69*(1), 157–173. doi:10.1111/j.1741-3737.2006.00351.x

Harpham, T., & Molyneux, C. (2001). Urban health in developing countries: A review. *Progress in Development Studies, 1*(2), 113–137.

National Bureau of Statistics of China. (2005). *China Statistical Yearbook 2005.* Beijing, China: National Bureau of Statistics of China.

National Bureau of Statistics of China. (2012). *China Statistical Yearbook 2012.* Retrieved from Beijing, China: National Bureau of Statistics of China.

National Bureau of Statistics of China. (2020a). *Size of the Rural-to-Urban Migration Till the End of the Second Quarter.* Retrieved from http://k.sina.com. cn/article_1655444627_62ac149302001gbuh.html?from=local

National Bureau of Statistics of China. (2013). *Statistical Communique of the People's Republic of China on the National Economic and Social Development in 2012.* Retrieved from http://www.stats.gov.cn/tjsj/tjgb/ndtjgb/qgndtjgb/20130 2/t20130221_30027.html

National Bureau of Statistics of China. (2010). *Tabulation on the 2010 Population Census of The People's Republic of China.* Retrieved from Beijing, China: National Bureau of Statistics of China.

National Bureau of Statistics of China. (2020b). *Tabulation on the Yearly Statistics of The People's Republic of China*. Retrieved from Beijing, China. https://data.st ats.gov.cn/easyquery.htm?cn=C01&zb=A0301&sj=2020

Quinn, A. (2008). Healthy aging in cities. *Journal of Urban Health, 85*(2), 151–153.

State Council of China. (2014). *China New Urbanization Planning (2014–2020)*. Retrieved from http://www.gov.cn/gongbao/content/2014/content_2644805.htm

Wainwright, N., & Surtees, P. (2002). Childhood adversity, gender and depression over the life-course. *Journal of Affective Disorders, 72*(1), 33–44. doi:10.1016/S0165-0327(01)00420-7

Wang, F. (2005). *Organizing Through Division and Exclusion: China's Hukou System*. Stanford, CA: Stanford University Press.

Wong, K., Fu, D., Li, C. Y., & Song, H. X. (2007). Rural migrant workers in urban China: Living a marginalised life. *International Journal of Social Welfare, 16*(1), 32–40. doi:10.1111/j.1468-2397.2007.00475.x

World Health Organization. (2007). *Global Age-Friendly Cities: A Guide*: Geneva, Switzerland: World Health Organization.

Zhang, K. H., & Song, S. (2003). Rural–urban migration and urbanization in China: Evidence from time-series and cross-section analyses. *China Economic Review, 14*(4), 386–400.

Zhang, L. (2008). Conceptualizing China's urbanization under reforms. *Habitat International, 32*(4), 452–470. doi:10.1016/j.habitatint.2008.01.001

2 Urbanization and depression of rural older population in China

History and typology of China's urbanization

According to the United Nations (1997), urbanization refers to the process in which the share of a population residing in an urban sector increases. It witnesses a large number of people becoming permanently concentrated in relatively small areas, forming cities. The implications for the process are multidimensional: economically, it means the booming of manufacturing and service industries, as well as the flourishing of consumption; demographically, it means massive migration from rural areas to urban areas, pursuing better life opportunities; socially, it results in profound social mobility, widening or bridging the gap between rich and poor; politically, it may promote the development of civil society, reshaping a nation's political texture substantially; and culturally, urbanization can bring diversity in terms of culture and lifestyle and pose challenges as well as opportunities to traditions (Marsella, 1998). Therefore, the process of urbanization represents a convergence of specific economic, population, social, political, and cultural forces, which can in turn affect individuals' mental health.

Though urbanization is closely associated with modernization, industrialization, and rationalization in literature, it is not a modern phenomenon. Looking back, it represents a rapid and historic transformation of human social roots on a global scale (Marsella, 1998). In the 19th century, Britain and several other European countries became the first urbanized countries after over a century of the process of urbanization. Since the late 20th century, developing countries have evolved into the main force behind the global urbanization trend (Girardet, 1996). According to Mokyr (1995), three urbanization types can be recognized in the history of world urbanization. The first is "parallel urbanization", meaning that urbanization is a result of industrial restructuring and technological advancement. The urbanization pattern applies to the current developed countries. In this pattern, cities promote the gains from trade and specialization through (1) providing a large enough market for products with cheaper prices but better

DOI: 10.4324/9781003248767-2

quality; and (2) providing desirable environments for the positive externalities and economies of scale and agglomeration.

The second type is "over-urbanization", referring to the fact that the speed of urbanization exceeds that of economic development. It usually happens in the developing world, where a sizeable urban labor force is not effectively employed or supported by the country's economic development. A notorious result is the emergence of slums. It is recognized that dependence on international capital contributes to the formation of this pattern. In the long run, this urbanization pattern hampers economic growth (Timberlake & Kentor, 1983).

The third is "under-urbanization", which is characterized by low levels of urbanization, state-controlled urban life, and the absence of a high-density central business district (CBD) and high-income, low-density residential suburbs. This pattern occurred in the socialist and post-socialist countries, and its characteristics persist to a certain degree, even when the country is transformed into a market-based economy (Scarpaci, 2000).

The above typology is made based on the dynamics of urbanization and economic development. Against this criterion, urbanization in contemporary China can be divided into two stages, with the Reform and Opening Up in the late 1970s as the watershed. Based on the typology of urbanization introduced above, pre-reform urbanization can be categorized as under-urbanization. This stage featured the domination of the state in economic development, including (1) hyperextension of state ownership; (2) highly centralized processes of making economic policy; (3) state-led forced industrialization and centrally planned mechanisms for accumulation; and (4) highly controlled rural-to-urban migration and the role of the city as an administrative and production center (Zhang, 2008).

On the other hand, however, post-reform urbanization in China does not fit into any one of the three urbanization types. The Chinese government has taken an encouraging attitude toward urbanization since the Reform, and urbanization in China has accelerated since the late 1990s, with more than half the population residing in the urban sector in 2011. According to the State Council of China (2014), the country is expected to have 100 million more people in the urban population by the end of 2020, and more small- to medium-sized cities will be developed from the current rural regions. Therefore, under-urbanization is no longer suitable to describe the situation in China. At the same time, due to the persistence of the *Hukou* system and the still preeminent role of the state in the national economy, China's urbanization is largely under political control and policy regulation. As such, it is also not appropriate to label it as over-urbanization or as parallel urbanization.

The features of urbanization in this stage can be four-fold: (1) in terms of ownership, though public ownership still has preponderance, private sector gets unprecedented development and the multiple ownership is introduced; (2) in terms of state role, the rights to make economic policies are decentralized to local governments which can be more entrepreneurial in making reforms; (3) in terms of mechanisms for accumulation, state monopoly is only found in key areas (e.g., major infrastructure industries and industries related to national security) and the market role expands substantially; and (4) cities become places with concentrations of commodity production and commercialized consumption (Zhang, 2008).

The evolution of urbanization in modern China can be represented by the urbanization policies introduced both in the pre-reform and post-reform periods. A summary of the representative policies can be found in Table 2.1. The introduction of the *Hukou* Regulations of China in 1958 set the tone for pre-reform urbanization policies, namely controlling the number of urban populations and cities. It strictly defined the social identity of Chinese people according to birthplace (i.e., born in a rural or in an urban area) and controlled migration between the rural and urban sectors (Wang, 2005). This orientation was initially switched in 1979, when the Central Committee of the Communist Party of China (CPC) decided to bridge the development gap between the rural and urban sectors. As a measure, the development of small cities and towns was proposed (Zhou & Ma, 2003).

In 1980, a national conference on urban planning was held, in which three urbanization principles were proposed, namely "control the size of mega cities", "rationally develop middle-size cities", and "promote the development of small cities and towns". These principles guided China's urbanization strategies in the following decades. The 1980s also witnessed the loosening of control over rural-to-urban population migration, which was symbolized by wider access to urban residences and by *Hukou* being allowed for rural residents. This transformation was mainly to satisfy the labor demand of the booming urban industries (Wang, 2005). Moreover, with the expansion of the population and of industry, China's urban sector had, since the 1980s, an increased need for land, when pilot reforms were initiated, as with the transfer of rights to the use of land (Yang & Wu, 1996).

Until the first decade of the new millennium, China saw a substantial decrease in institutional obstacles to rural population migration and land use. On the one hand, rural people have wider access to opportunities to change their social identity traditionally defined by the *Hukou* status. This has encouraged massive out-migration from the countryside, mainly comprising young laborers, which in turn has a profound influence on rural living arrangements. On the other hand, with the legalization of land transfer and the trading of the rights to the use of land, rural communities obtained

Table 2.1 China's major urbanization policies in the pre-reform and post-reform period

Year	Urbanization policy text	Urbanization policy objectives
1958	"*Hukou* Regulations of China"	Strict control on rural-to-urban migration
1963	"Instruction on Urban Institution Adjustment and Suburban Area Shrinkage"	Decrease of cities and urban population
1979	"CPC's Decisions on Promoting Agricultural Development"	Bridge urban–rural gap and develop small cities and towns
1980	"Report of National Urban Planning Conference"	Control the size of mega cities; rationally develop middle-size cities; and promote the development of small cities and towns
1984	"State Council's Announcement on Peasants' Access to Urban Residence and Hukou"	The restrictions on rural-to-urban migration were loosened
1995	"Several Propositions on Promoting the Development of Small Cities and Townships"	Initiating the comprehensive reform of small cities and towns
1998	"Regulations for Enforcing the Land Management Law"	The right to the use of land can be transferred from the state and collective
2008	"CPC's Decisions on Promoting Rural Reform and Development"	Rural land transfer was accepted
2010	"CPC Conference on Economic Affairs"	Urbanization is pivotal for further economic reform
2014	"China New Urbanization Planning"	People-centered urbanization; citizenship rights
2019	"Instructions on Developing Modern Metropolitan Areas"	Remove institutional obstacles for the free flow of essential productive factors; build world-class metropolitan areas

the spatial, social, and economic resources to restructure the environment. Related activities mainly include infrastructure building, industry development, and welfare enhancement, which aims to restructure a community's physical and socioeconomic environment (Guo, 2001).

Since 2010, especially after the formation of the Xi Jinping–Li Keqiang Administration, urbanization has been promoted as the pivot for China's deepening economic reform. Institutional obstacles are further decreased. This can be reflected in the reform of the *Hukou* system and the proposition of "people-centered urbanization" on the one hand (State Council of China, 2014); and on the other hand, the deepening pilot reforms have accumulated lessons and experience on developing small cities and towns.

Analysis of the development path reveals the exogenous nature of China's urbanization, namely Chinese urbanization is largely state-led and policy-driven. At the same time, the multidimensionality of the effects of urbanization found elsewhere also applies to China. From the health perspective, Gong et al. (2012) found that urbanization can affect Chinese people through population migration, healthcare delivery, lifestyle change, environmental pollution and alteration, and population aging. That is, the risk factors resulting from urbanization can be displayed at the individual, household, and community levels. Hence, a comprehensive analysis framework is needed to guide the investigation into the multidimensionality of the influences of urbanization in China.

2.1 Social determinants of older people's mental health

One's mental health is shaped to a great extent by various social, economic, and physical environments operating at different life stages (Allen, Balfour, Bell, & Marmot, 2014). Differences in mental health have been consistently recorded for people of different gender, age, ethnicity, education, income, and geographic area of residence (World Health Organization and Calouste Gulbenkian Foundation, 2014). Epidemiological studies have reported that a number of socio-demographic features are associated with common mental disorders (depression and anxiety), including being female, older in age, low educational attainment, weak social support, and social isolation (Fryers, Melzer, & Jenkins, 2003; Lehtinen, Sohlman, & Kovess-Masfety, 2005; Lund et al., 2010). From an economic aspect, low socioeconomic status, such as being materially disadvantaged and unemployed, is a significant risk factor for mental health (Jenkins et al., 2008; Patel et al., 2010). Moreover, environmental conditions, such as housing and community infrastructure availability, were also found to be important for mental health and can often reduce the risks associated with mental disorders and poor mental health (Turley, Saith, Bhan, Rehfuess, & Carter, 2013; Wright & Kloos, 2007).

It is also worth noting that disadvantages in terms of mental health from the social, economic, and environmental aspects can emerge before birth and accumulate throughout one's lifetime (Kelly, Sacker, Del Bono, Francesconi, & Marmot, 2011). Strong evidence shows that many mental health problems emerge in later life but originate in early life (Fryers & Brugha, 2013; Shonkoff et al., 2012). Therefore, a comprehensive framework that encompasses a perspective that looks into the different levels of social determinants for mental health, as well as taking life stages into account, will be applied to understanding the social determinants for mental health. In a nutshell, it will be a "person-process-context" framework.

This comprehensive framework still receives little attention in mental health studies on the Chinese rural population. As the most important contextual feature for rural China now, urbanization is leading to profound changes in social, economic, and physical environments that may affect the mental health of Chinese rural populations both in a positive and in a negative way. At the individual level, it can change the social identity of rural residents, namely from rural residence booklet (i.e., the rural *Hukou*) holder to urban residence booklet (i.e., the urban *Hukou*) holder. This identity change means not only wider access to public resources, such as welfare benefits and job opportunities, but also higher social prestige. At the household level, urbanization has resulted in a shift in family living arrangements in the countryside. Working-age people migrate into the cities, leaving their underage children and older family members behind in the rural hometown. This means weak social support as well as more care responsibilities, if not burdens, for the rural population. At the community level, land expropriation resulting from urbanization can substantially transform the socioeconomic and physical environment of a rural community. It can lead to enhanced infrastructure, new ways of interacting, and job opportunities in industries other than agriculture for rural community-based residents. These urbanization-led social changes, bringing both risks and opportunities, have rarely been discussed in a structured way, and no comprehensive picture has been outlined with regard to their implications for rural mental health in the context of China. Based on the basic characteristics and development trends of China's urbanization, therefore, the following three background factors will be taken into account when examining the mental health of the rural older population.

2.1.1 *Life-course context for the mental health of the aging population*

According to the World Health Organization and Calouste Gulbenkian Foundation (2014), it is important to investigate how various risk factors in the formative stages of one's life influence mental health or gradually lead to mental disorders many years or even decades later in life. This is especially true for the aging population, whose human development outcomes can be shaped by social determinants in the prenatal, pregnancy, and perinatal periods, early childhood, adolescence, working and family-building years, and the older ages. Take social institutions and arrangements as an example. The education and social care one receives, and the work one performs, fundamentally affect one's capabilities to choose one's own course in life. Experience of these social institutions and arrangements differs enormously and their structures and impacts are, to a greater or lesser extent, influenced or mitigated by public policies. As such, it is suggested that systematic and comprehensive action should be taken across one's life course to maintain mental wellbeing, and giving every child the best possible start will result in desirable mental health benefits for later life (Cherlin, Chase-Lansdale, & McRae, 1998).

Significant life events happening at birth may affect one's mental health across a lifetime. Roseboom et al. (2006) found that the babies born in Dutch Famine years were smaller in size and more likely to have a higher risk of chronic disease in later life, which in turn became stressors of mental health. The association of prenatal malnutrition and poorer health has also been recorded in many other studies (e.g., Painter et al., 2006; Painter, Roseboom, and Bleker,2005). Disadvantages at birth can also impose a direct effect on mental health in later life. Jones et al. (1998) reported that abnormalities in pregnancy, delivery, and the neonatal period were associated with adult-onset schizophrenia. A number of studies also demonstrated that exposure to the Chinese Famine of 1959–1961 was associated with a much higher risk of schizophrenia (Brown & Susser, 2008; Song, Wang, & Hu, 2009).

The long arm of some family and school experiences in the childhood period can reach into old age. For instance, the experience or witness of domestic violence is significantly associated with mental and behavioral disorders in adulthood and old age (Edwards, Holden, Felitti, & Anda, 2003). Other forms of childhood maltreatment within the family, such as neglect and sexual abuse, have also been demonstrated to have lifelong effects on an individual's mental health (Spataro, Mullen, Burgess, Wells, & Moss, 2004). The behavioral traits of parents at this period may also affect one's later-life mental wellbeing. Studies have demonstrated that having an alcoholic or violent parent before adulthood is significantly associated with depression in adulthood (Anda et al., 2002).

Many life events in the youth and middle-aged periods, such as marriage and divorce, employment and unemployment, and having a child, are closely associated with mental health at old age (Brown, Bulanda, & Lee, 2005; Horwitz & White, 1998). It is worth noting that actions taken in the life-course transitional periods can be of special significance for mental health in the following life stages: for instance, retirement planning in advance and bridge employment predict less depression at old age (Topa, Moriano, Depolo, Alcover, & Morales, 2009).

With specific attention to the childhood period, existing studies have ambivalent findings as to the association between childhood adversity and mental health in later life. There are many types of childhood adversity: in terms of family background and family relationship, it may include financial strain, parental illiteracy or low education, divorce or separation of parents, internal abuse, witness of domestic violence, and the deaths of close family members; in terms of health and function, it may include poor physical health, chronic diseases, and disabilities; in terms of the social and political context, it may include war, famine, and other traumatic experiences. Mainly based on the life-course framework, past literature found that childhood adversities (CAs) could be associated with the onset of mental problems all through one's life (e.g., Green et al., 2010; Wainwright and Surtees, 2002). Two explanations have been proposed for the correlation. One is in relation to the depressive personality. That is, adverse experience in childhood may shape a depressive personality that persists one's whole life (Kasen et al., 2001). The other is guided by the theory of cumulative disadvantage. It holds that CAs can evolve into low social supports and socioeconomic status in adult life, which in turn become risks of depression (Chen et al., 2005).

On the contrary, some other researchers reported that CAs were not significantly associated with poorer psychological wellbeing in adult life. In some circumstances, they may result in better psychological states. Related examples include the successful adaptation in later life and the stronger life resilience of adolescent mothers (Black & Ford-Gilboe, 2004), of adults who survived the traumatic war in Cambodia all through the 1970s (Fergusson & Horwood, 2003), and troubled teenagers and delinquent youths (Werner & Smith, 2001). The perspectives of protective process and compensatory process were utilized to illustrate the findings. On the one hand, some studies reported that resilience factors, including personality, gender, problem-solving skills, intelligence, parental attachment, parenting skills, and peer affiliation, can offset or even reverse the negative mental health effects of CAs (Fergusson & Horwood, 2003; Werner & Smith, 2001). On the other hand, the significance of CAs on depression was found to attenuate in magnitude with the life-course stage (Collishaw et al., 2007; Green et al., 2010).

The controversies over the effects of CAs on adult depressive symptoms can be due to two reasons. The first one is in relation to the method used to analyze CAs. Past literature investigated CAs as independent life events. That is to say, many existing studies either only focused on one type of CA or examined CAs one by one. This methodology may largely ignore the interrelationship and combined effects between CAs, let alone their typology. An increasing body of literature has demonstrated that CAs are highly correlated with each other. For instance, children born in a family with poor social and economic resources are more likely to leave school early and have poorer physical health (Bradley & Corwyn, 2002); and children who have witnessed or experienced family abuse or parental divorce were found more likely to commit crime in adolescence and thus be punished by legal institutions (Demuth & Brown, 2004). Therefore, CAs can come about hand in hand or be cumulative along the life course, which necessitates a clustered examination of CAs. A clustered methodology can avoid overestimating associations involving a particular CA on the one hand and information negligence on the other (Kessler, Davis, & Kendler, 1997).

Second, few studies have been found that examine the life events that happen between the childhood and the later-life stages, such as those in relation to socioeconomic status transformation. This can also lead to ambivalent findings with regard to the effects of childhood adversity on later-life depressive symptoms. In China's context, urbanization has been the most significant social background for the socioeconomic status transformation of rural people in the past three decades. For rural residents, obtaining an urban *Hukou* not only means access to essential social resources and welfare benefits, but also detaching from the social stigma of rurality (Wang, 2001). Due to more job opportunities and higher income, even living in the urban sector without holding an urban *Hukou* can be an advantage compared with staying in the countryside. Since urbanization is a social transformation taking place after the childhood stage for the current Chinese rural mature and older population, taking into account the identity transformation that happens in the urbanization process can make clear the association between childhood adversity and later-life depressive symptoms.

It is also worth noting that although some family-related CAs showed a particular significance for depressive symptoms in adulthood (Green et al., 2010), they can be socially or culturally specific. For instance, Chinese society's attitude toward marriage was rather conservative before the Reform and Opening Up in the late 1970s, especially in the rural sector, which made divorce a rare occurrence at that period (Liao & Heaton, 1992). As such, divorce of parents is a CA experienced by few current Chinese mature and older adults. Further, China, in its modern history, had not had a stable social and political environment until the late 1970s. That is, constant and turbulent wars and political upheaval could have exacerbated the negative effects of natural disasters and result in massive famines. The Great Chinese Famine that happened between 1959 and 1961 is a notorious example. Smil (1999) estimated that the famine resulted in some 30 million deaths and about the same number of birth losses or postponements. Therefore, famine should be taken into consideration when investigating the CAs of the Chinese mature and older population.

Moreover, for an aging population, the trajectory of socioeconomic status transformation in earlier life stages has significant mental health implications. Luo and Waite (2005) found that on the one hand both childhood and adult socioeconomic status are important for health; and on the other hand, the negative impact of low childhood socioeconomic status can be buffered by the higher status in adulthood.

2.1.2 Household context for the mental health of the aging population

Many of the mental health problems in the aging population are associated with the family context (Fiori, Antonucci, & Cortina, 2006). The most direct association is from the hereditary nature of mental disorders. Many mental illnesses, including depression, run in families, which suggests that they can be passed from parents to children through the genes. However, existing literature is still debating about which factor, environment or heredity, plays the more important role in the cause of mental disorders (Kendler et al., 1995).

From the perspective of family relations, Repetti, Taylor, and Seeman (2002) defined the characteristics of a family presenting a risk for mental and physical health. These characteristics include aggressiveness, cold relationships, unsupportiveness, and neglectfulness between family members. The authors held that these negative features could lead to vulnerabilities and/or interact with genetically based vulnerabilities in one's mental wellbeing, which in turn damage one's psychosocial functioning stress-responsive biological regulatory systems, as well as lead to poor health behaviors, such as substance and alcohol abuse. Some other studies have also demonstrated that the integrated biobehavioral profile of a family leads to consequent accumulation of risk for mental health disorder, major chronic disease, and early mortality (Sander & McCarty, 2005; Tolan, Gorman-Smith, Huesmann, & Zelli, 1997).

Further, family living arrangements can be both an antecedent and a result of family relations, and thus have significant mental health implications (Ye & Chen, 2014). Though the cultures of the living arrangements of aging populations may vary between countries in the world, co-residence with family members, such as spouse and adult children, usually means a successful aging style, especially in the context of East Asian countries (Zhan, 2004). Reasons can be given from an instrumentalist perspective and a cultural perspective. On the one hand, living with other family members guarantees emotional and material support. That is, older people are more likely to have feelings of being cared about and being loved, of security, and of emotional stability when living in a coresident family (Ha, 2008). On the other hand, some traditional cultures, such as Confucianism in China, encourage a multi-generational family and harmony between family members (Bian, Logan, & Bian, 1998). At the same time, however, some literature has reported that the co-residence of family members could be a significant predictor of mental disorder in older people. Life stressors, such as the burden of care and domestic conflict, are more likely to take place in a multi-generational family, which can result in or worsen the poor mental health of older family members (Patel & Prince, 2001; Pinquart & Sörensen, 2003).

The significance of family context on mental health is also reflected in the aspect of family socioeconomic status (SES). According to Louis and Zhao (2002), family SES may to a large extent determine the mental well-being of a child and the effect can persist until adulthood and later life. As suggested by the literature, economic deprivation in the family significantly predicts poorer mental health. However, the evidence for the mental health advantage of ample family economic resources is ambivalent. Some studies proposed that it was not the family economic resources per se but how they are used that affects people's mental health (Axinn, Duncan, & Thornton, 1997).

In current-day China, the family context for the mental health of the rural aging population has been substantially changed in the urbanization process, which is mainly reflected in the household living-arrangement shift (i.e., spatial separation between family members). The existing literature has well documented the implications of family spatial separation on the mental health of the aging population (Hank, 2007; Smith, 1998). However, few of them were conducted in the context of developing countries (Guo, Aranda, & Silverstein, 2009), where the causes of family separation, family structure, and the economic and cultural traits of the aging population can be different from those in the developed countries. In China's urbanization, massive rural-to-urban population migration has resulted in separation of hundreds of millions of youth laborers and their family members, represented by the increased share of "empty-nest" and "skipped-generation" households in the countryside (Du, Ding, Li, & Gui, 2004). This is a substantial deviation from the traditional Chinese rural household living arrangement that featured the co-residence of multiple generations. The prevalence of economic considerations, at the same time as traditional family values recede, may result in significant mental health implications for the rural aging population. This can be especially true in rural China, where the public services and welfare arrangements are still underdeveloped.

The effects of the migration of the children's generation on the elderly left behind have been discussed mainly from the resources perspective. That is, children's out-migration affects informal support resources of the elderly parents who remain (Guo et al., 2009). The informal supports comprise instrumental support (i.e., hands-on support with personal care and housework), monetary and in-kind support, and emotional support. The effects of out-migration on them may vary. First, the instrumental support tends to diminish due to the absence of the younger generation. According to the theory of modernization and aging, urbanization and industrialization is associated with decreased old-age care, mainly due to the increased geographical distance between generations and decreased family orientation (Aboderin, 2004; Kuhn, 2005). Second, the monetary and in-kind support will increase due to the remittances from out-migrated children. In China and other Asian countries where family collectivism and filial obligation are prevalent, migrated children tend to compensate for the non-fulfillment of family responsibilities by sending back remittances regularly (Du, Park, & Wang, 2005; Imai, Gaiha, Ali, & Kaicker, 2014).

Third, the findings with regard to emotional support transformation after child migration are inconsistent. On the one hand, some studies reported that out-migration of children decreases the emotional support for the parents left behind and makes them more susceptible to stress-related health problems such as hypertension, and to psychological distress such as depressive symptoms (Lu, 2012; Silver, 2014). On the other hand, other studies, mainly based on the East Asian context, reported that the family emotional connection did not diminish along with the out-migration of family members. The reasons are two-fold. First, the location of children may not be the best way of judging the support of elderly parents, and most migrant children were found to be still providing long-distance emotional support, such as regular contact by telephone (Baldock, 2000; Kreager, 2006). Second, non-migrant children and other family members may compensate for the loss of emotional support. Guo et al. (2009) have stressed the importance of taking a holistic perspective to look into the change in emotional support resulting from migration. It is held that the majority of older people in Asia still live close to at least one of their children and the non-migrant children can be an alternative support resource (Beard & Kunharibowo, 2001; Frankenberg, Chan, & Ofstedal, 2002). Therefore, the out-migration of children may affect the mental health of parents left behind through the pathways in relation to instrumental support, monetary support, and emotional support, and the significance of each pathway may vary.

2.1.3 Community context for the mental health of the aging population

Past literature has shown consistent evidence with regard to the significant effects of community-level factors on the mental health of the aging population. These factors include the community built environment, socioeconomic status, and cohesion. First, the community built environment has both direct and indirect effects on mental health (Evans, 2003). The direct effects come from high-rise housing, poor-quality housing, improper design, aa high level of stimulation, low walkability, noise, air pollution, residential over-crowding, and insufficient daylight (Araya et al., 2006; Evans, 2003; Weich et al., 2002). The indirect effects come from the association between the built environment and personal control, socially supportive relationships, and recovery from stress and fatigue (Northridge, Sclar, & Biswas, 2003). These significant associations in turn affect community-based residents' mental wellbeing. According to Evans (2003), the effects of the commu-nity built environment on mental health are independent and are beyond the effects of the individuals' personal stressors, such as poverty and negative life events.

Second, low community socioeconomic status is also a significant stressor for individual mental health. Communities with low socioeco-nomic status feature high poverty, crime, and unemployment rate, and a large volume of studies have demonstrated the associations between these disadvantages and mental disorders, such as major depression and anxiety (Hill, Ross, & Angel, 2005; Ross & Mirowsky, 2001). According to Robert (1998), although factors in relation to community socioeconomic status have less significant effect on individual mental health than those in rela-tion to individual and family socioeconomic status, they can make worse the harmful impact of personal stressors and interfere with the formation of bonds between people, again increasing risks of depression (Cutrona, Wallace, & Wesner, 2006). Also, low community socioeconomic status does not influence all residents in the same way, since people have different personality traits (Evans, 2003). Usually, low community socioeconomic status means limited social and public resources, including the services and funding for mental health, which is another risk factor for residents' mental wellbeing (Mickus, Colenda, & Hogan, 2014).

Third, community cohesion is also a significant predictor for the men-tal health of the aging population. Community cohesion implies the ways community residents relate to and provide support for each other, which is closely related to access to resources like social support and social capi-tal (Obasaju, Palin, Jacobs, Anderson, & Kaslow, 2009). In real-life situa-tions, it usually refers to informal social ties in the community. According to Gapen et al. (2011), low community cohesion can exacerbate the situa-tion of persons with post-traumatic stress disorder; while high community cohesion is likely to buffer the negative effects of neighborhood disorder on residents' mental health. It is also worth noting that community cohesion is a result of the increased level of friendship/acquaintanceship ties and the decreased level of anonymity among residents (Sampson, 1991), and voluntary organizations in the community are a major contributor to community cohesion (Skogan, 1989).

In rural China, the community context for the mental health of the aging population is mainly shaped by land expropriation resulting from urbanization. China's urbanization in the past more than three decades features massive amounts of land in rural communities being expropriated and developed for non-agricultural usage (Cohen, 2006; Frumkin, Frank, & Jackson, 2004). China's urban space increased by 74.6% between 2000 and 2011, and the government initiated an ambitious urbanization scheme in 2014 which set out to increase the urban population by 100 million and facilitate the development of more towns and small- to medium-sized cities with modern infrastructures by 2020 (State Council of China, 2014). This means more land will be expropriated from Chinese rural communities in the foreseeable future.

Land expropriation in rural China has proceeded at a remarkable scale since the late 1980s, when the recession of agriculture and financial pressure on local government administration prompted a fervent growth of "development zones" (Guo, 2001). The unique land system makes land expropriation in China "government behavior". That is, the Chinese government owns all the land in the country and it can legally manipulate coercive measures to acquire land from individuals at the expense of some discretionary compensatory arrangements; on the other hand, rural farmers can only have the right to use and supervise the land assigned by a village collective. Therefore, from a legal perspective, the state expropriates land from the village collective, namely the rural community, rather than from individuals. The user's right to the expropriated land, then, will be sold according to the market value, and the returns belong to the government.

A portion of the returns from land-use rights transfer will be appropriated to the village collective as compensation, which will in turn be directed to the individual farmers. For thousands of years, arable land has been the fundamental base for the life of rural residents, and the loss of it means essential changes in their occupation, income, and ways of living and interacting (Ilbery, 2014). At the same time, the effects of land expropriation on individuals can also be imposed through the change in the rural community environment. The expropriated land is mainly used for real estate development, infrastructure construction, and industrial usage (Guo, 2001). As such, it usually brings in enhanced infrastructure and a proportion of non-agricultural industry for the affected rural community. The modernization of the rural community is also reflected in the social aspect: real estate development attracts urban residents and alters the pattern of inhabitants;

transitions of industry structure require the upgrading of public services; and with increased income and more access to urban culture and lifestyles, rural people tend to socialize and interact in a way different from the traditional style. As a result, the self-sufficient peasant economy weakens while the market-based non-agricultural industries develop; the traditional acquaintance society declines while grassroots organizations for hobbies and mutual help flourish. These changes in the physical and socioeconomic aspects of Chinese rural community can significantly affect the mental health of community-based residents.

Existing literature has ambivalent findings with regard to the mental health implications of the community restructuring resulting from urban expansion. On the one hand, rural community restructuring can lead to a stressful lifestyle, a polluted environment, and adaptation to changes that impose negative effects on mental health (Chen, Chen, & Landry, 2013; Gong et al., 2012; Harpham & Molyneux, 2001). On the other hand, it can confer positive effects by expanding employment opportunities and movement of people and capital (Fraser et al., 2005), or just be a non-significant predictor of mental health (Sturm & Cohen, 2004). Moreover, little related literature is based in the developing world, whose urban expansion process, and thus community restructuring, is different from that of the developed countries in terms of driving forces and the socioeconomic features of affected populations (Cohen, 2004; Couch, Leontidou, & Petschel-Held, 2007). As such, the findings from the Western world may not be applied to the developing economies. It is also worth noting that rural community restructuring is in the context of global population aging. Due to the rapidly aging population in developing countries, facilitating effective public health strategies for reducing depressive symptoms will be a health issue of priority in rural community restructuring schemes.

2.2 Risk factors and consequences of mental health problems for older adults

Prevalence of mental health problems may increase with rising age. According to Phillips et al. (2009), prevalence rate of DSM-IV axis I disorder was 12.51%, 23.23%, and 24.04% for the age group of 18–39 years, 40–54 years, and 55 years or above, respectively, in China. The most common mental disorders for the Chinese mature and older population, in order of prevalence, are mood disorders, such as depression; anxiety disorders, such as panic disorder and post-traumatic stress disorder; substance use disorder, mainly alcohol use disorder; and psychotic disorders, such as schizophrenia (Phillips et al., 2009). However, some studies suggest that mental disorders are underreported in China, especially in the older population (Ng, 1997; Yang & Kleinman, 2008). Various social risk factors for mental health may appear in the process of aging, and an increasing body of literature has focused on how these factors affect the mature and older population.

First, the decline in physical and functional health may increase the social risk factors for mental health. The existing literature consistently reports that physical health and function tend to deteriorate with rising age (Kulminski et al., 2006; Mitnitski & Rockwood, 2006; Yashin, Ukraintseva, Boiko, & Arbeev, 2002), taking the form of increased incidence and prevalence of chronic diseases (e.g., hypertension and diabetes), functional loss in hearing or vision, and disabilities in activities of daily living (ADL) or instrumental activities of daily living (IADL). It is noted that decreased physical and functional health usually means increased need for care assistance and thus dependency on other people. This is especially true for those middle-aged and older persons' ADL or IADL disabilities after a fall, stroke, or heart failure. The rapid loss of functional autonomy can be detrimental to self-efficacy and lead to depression (Hellstrom, Lindmark, Wahlberg, & Fugl-Meyer, 2003).

It is also worth noting that one's health is influenced by the health of one's spouse (Christakis & Allison, 2006). As such, studies on the association between functional and health decline and mental health pay attention to couple-level evidence. Some studies have reported that a spouse's functional disability and chronic diseases can affect middle-aged and older people's depressive symptoms (Fultz et al., 2005; Siegel, Bradley, Gallo, & Kasl, 2004).

Second, bereavement is also a significant risk factor for the depression of the aging population. The loss of loved ones (e.g., spouse and other close family members, friends, or even a pet) is usually unavoidable in the process of aging for the mature and older population. It is always associated with psychological and functional impairment. In most cases, the bereavement process eventually results in restored psychological equilibrium after a certain period of time; while in some other cases, it can become severe and evolve into complicated grief or prolonged grief (Kersting, Brähler, Glaesmer, & Wagner, 2011). It is reported that the prevalence rate of complicated grief and subthreshold complicated grief can reach 2.4% and 22.7%, respectively, among middle-aged and older people with bereavement (Fujisawa et al., 2010). At the same time, various factors, such as the quality of relationship with the deceased, circumstances of the death, availability of social support, and original mental health state, can play an important role in mental impairment after a loss (Kersting et al., 2011).

Third, the decline in socioeconomic status (SES) along with the aging process may increase the risks of depression. SES is usually measured as a combination of education, income, and occupation, differentiations of which show inequalities in access to and distribution of various resources. Among the three components, people in later-life stages can experience decline in income and occupation status in the process of aging, especially after their retirement. Statistics show that the prevalence rate of poverty is significantly higher in the older population than in other age groups, and this is especially true for older females (Förster & Mira D'Ercole, 2005; Gornick, Munzi, Sierminska, & Smeeding, 2009). In the context of China, the prevalence rate in the older population is three times that of the general population (Yang, 2011). Economic vulnerability along the aging process can be a result of increased medical and care expenses, withdrawal from the labor market, loss of life support, and limited income resources (Brady, 2004; Gornick et al., 2009).

A large volume of literature has demonstrated that low SES in later life is significantly associated with mental health problems. For instance, withdrawal from the job market is usually accompanied by a drop in self-efficacy, which can evolve into chronic stress (Butterworth et al., 2006); low SES is also associated with low subjective wellbeing in later life, and income is correlated more strongly with wellbeing than is education (Pinquart & Sörensen, 2000).

Good mental health is integral to human health and wellbeing. It enables people to do and be things they have reasons to value. Therefore, problems in mental health can have significant effects on people's lives. This is especially true of depressive symptoms. When depressive symptoms reach a certain intensity and frequency, a person will be diagnosed as suffering from clinical depression that interferes with one's ability to work, sleep, study, eat, and enjoy life (American Psychiatric Association, 2013). Past literature reveals that depression in later life is a major public health concern (Serby & Yu, 2003) and there is consistent evidence showing that depression leads to increased risks of problems in physical health, functional autonomy, behavior, and social relationships in the mature and older population.

Depression has comorbidity to a number of physical health problems by affecting the digestive, immune, vascular, and nervous systems in the human body. It affects people's appetite and increases the risk of eating disorders. Either overeating or losing one's appetite can lead to many health problems, such as obesity, type 2 diabetes, stomachaches, cramps, constipation, and malnutrition, and the symptoms of these illnesses may not be improved by medication (Stice & Shaw, 2004). Depression weakens one's immune system, adding to vulnerability to infection and disease (Dantzer,

O'Connor, Freund, Johnson, & Kelley, 2008). It can also speed heart rate and constrict blood vessels, and this can lead to heart disease in the long run (Musselman, Evans, & Nemeroff, 1998). Moreover, by affecting the nervous system, it can cause headaches, chronic body aches, and pain that may not respond to medication (Hooten, Shi, Gazelka, & Warner, 2011).

According to the World Health Organization and Calouste Gulbenkian Foundation (2014), depression is the second leading cause of disability worldwide. It results in great suffering and leads to functional impairment in daily life, which is especially true for an aging population. Studies have not only shown that older people with depressive symptoms are more likely to have functional disability (Penninx, Leveille, Ferrucci, Van Eijk, & Guralnik, 1999), but also tend to have lower functional status compared to those with chronic medical conditions such as lung disease, hypertension, or diabetes (World Health Organization, 2012). And the comorbidities of depression and chronic diseases can be especially harmful for people's functional health (Egede, 2004). Depression also increases the perception of poor health, the utilization of medical services, and healthcare costs (World Health Organization, 2012). At the same time, statistics have also shown that depression is a major contributor to the global burden of disease, with major depressive disorder (MDD) accounting for 85% of years lived with disabilities (YLDs) and disability-adjusted life years (DALYs) (Ferrari et al., 2013). According to Reddy (2010), the negative effects of depression on function could be especially serious in the developing world.

Depression can be a significant predictor of many behavioral problems. If left untreated, depression can finally lead to suicide. Among all age groups, the older population has the highest suicidal rate. Statistics from different countries showed that as many as 90% of suicides or suicide attempts in the older population were significantly associated with depression (Alexopoulos, 2005). Therefore, many studies have suggested that special attention should be given to older people with long-term depression (Vanderhorst & McLaren, 2005). Moreover, depression can result in some other self-harm behaviors, like self-injuring or inflicting pain upon oneself with methods like cutting or burning (Martinez et al., 2005). People with depression are also more likely to have addictions. According to Nunes and Levin (2004), in order to alleviate the symptoms, depressed people tend to self-medicate with substances or to abuse alcohol, which increases the chances of getting addicted. Other reckless behaviors, such as driving drunk and unprotected sex, are also more prevalent among people with depression (Hubicka, Källmén, Hiltunen, & Bergman, 2010; Morokoff et al., 2009). In a nutshell, the behavioral problems resulting from depression can further lead to other significant public health concerns.

People with depression are likely to have more problems in social and familial relationships. On the one hand, due to aggressiveness and recklessness in behaviors, depressed people can lash out with violent emotions in front of family members and friends (Wang & Zhao, 2012). This can lead to tense or alienated relations between family members, especially between generations. With regard to an aging population, a problematic intergenerational relation can in turn affect psychological wellbeing significantly (Katz, 2009). On the other hand, depressed people can go to another extreme, namely that of isolating themselves (Cornwell & Waite, 2009). In the long run, depression leaves people drained emotionally, mentally, and physically, so it becomes hard for there to be friends and family around. The negative consequences of depression have also been reported in life satisfaction, job satisfaction and performance, and cognitive function (Katz, 2009; Moon & Hur, 2011; Nunes & Levin, 2004).

2.3 The mental health of the Chinese rural older population

Mental health problem is a significant public health concern for the Chinese rural population. Between 1982 and 2009, four major epidemiological surveys on mental health were carried out in China, namely the Mental Illness Epidemiological Study in Twelve Regions of China in 1982, the Mental Illness Epidemiological Study in Seven Provinces of China in 1993, the World Mental Health Survey in urban Beijing and Shanghai in 2002, and the Mental Health Epidemiological Study in Four City-Provinces in 2009 (Huang et al., 2019). Only the former two covered rural populations. Utilizing the International Classification of Diseases-9 (ICD-9), the 1982 study and the 1993 study reported that the lifetime prevalence of mental disorders in rural China was 9.88‰ and 11.61‰, respectively (Huang, 2008). Applying the same screening tool, a number of local epidemiological surveys recorded the mental illness prevalence rate of the rural population in certain prefectures or provinces in later years: the survey in Shantou in 1995 reported 14.06‰ (Lin et al., 1998), the survey in Zhongshan in 2000 reported 27.52‰ (Hu, Li, & Chen, 2002), the survey in Jiangxi in 2002 reported 32.85‰ (Chen, Hu, & Chen, 2004), and the survey in Guangzhou in 2006 reported 37.30‰ (Zhao, Huang, & Li, 2009). These studies together may predict an increasingly higher prevalence rate of mental illness in rural China.

Only in 2012 did China launch its first nationally representative survey on mental health, namely the China Mental Health Survey (CMHS). The CMHS conducted face-to-face interviews with 32,552 adult respondents

from 157 nationwide representative population-based disease sur-
veillance points in 31 provinces across China. It applied a two-stage
design by trained lay interviewers and psychiatrists with the Composite
International Diagnostic Interview, the Structured Clinical Interview
for DSM-IV Axis I disorders, the Community Screening Instrument for
Dementia from the 10/66 dementia diagnostic package, and the Geriatric
Mental State Examination. The survey revealed that the 12-month prevalence for any disorders (excluding dementia) in rural China was 13.4%,
significantly higher than that for the urban population (5.5%) (Huang
et al., 2019).

Mental health disparities between Chinese rural and urban populations
are worthy of more attention. Utilizing the Structured Clinical Interview
for Diagnostic and Statistical Manual (DSM)-IV axis I disorders, Phillips
et al. (2009) carried out a mental disorders epidemiological survey in four
Chinese provinces between 2001 and 2005. The sampling frame of this
survey included 12% of the adult population in China. The study reported
that the prevalence rate for major depressive disorder, dysthymic disorder,
alcohol dependence, and other mental disorders (including somatoform disorders, adjustment disorder, and hypochondriasis) were significantly higher
in rural areas than in urban areas (Phillips et al., 2009). Local studies based
in Guangzhou, Jiangxi, Hebei, and Zhejiang also reported a higher mental
illness prevalence rate in rural China (Chen et al., 2004; Li, Cui, & Cui,
2007; Shi, Zhang, & Xu, 2005).

Researching into the mental health of Chinese rural older people has
significant social implications. China is aging rapidly, and most of its older
population reside in the countryside. However, the life quality of this population is hampered by relatively lower levels of healthcare services, infrastructure, and pension schemes in the rural sector, which in turn imposes
negative influences on their mental health. The mental health disadvantages
of Chinese rural older adults have been revealed in some nationally representative surveys. For instance, China Health and Retirement Longitudinal
Study (CHARLS), a national representative survey launched by the
National School of Development in Peking University, reported the disadvantages of rural mature and older people in social support, leisure-time
activities, and depressive symptoms (Yang & Lou, 2016). It is worth noting
that nearly half of rural older people did not have any leisure-time activities,
according to the CHARLS datasets. For those who had, the activities were
highly homogeneous: mostly playing Ma-jong, chess, or cards. Moreover,
it is revealed that social support for them has largely been weakened, due
to the out-migration of younger generations. This in turn enhances risks of
depression for them.

The existing literature explains the mental health disparity in rural and urban China mainly through economic and public policy perspectives, while other aspects of social determinants are understudied. In other words, the mental health disadvantages in the rural sector are largely attributed to a lower level of economic development, fewer job opportunities, and poorer mental health services provision (Patel & Kleinman, 2003; Licheng Zhang, Wang, Wang, & Hsiao, 2006). However, the World Health Organization and Calouste Gulbenkian Foundation (2014) pointed out that the social determinants for mental health are multidimensional, and are embedded in the social, economic, and physical environments people are attached to. Therefore, a comprehensive perspective should be adopted to understand the depression of older adults in rural China by examining the inequalities in social, economic, and physical environments. Moreover, the border between rural and urban in contemporary China is far from stationary due to the vast urbanization process. Along with the expansion of urban populations and areas, profound changes are taking place in physical and socioeconomic environments, which can bring risks as well as opportunities to the mental health of Chinese rural older population. Therefore, there are urgent needs to examine the social determinants of elderly depression in the context of urbanization.

2.4 Summary

This chapter reviews the literature on urbanization and how it associates to the mental health of people. Moreover, it reviews the consequences of mental health problems, especially depression, for older adults in the context of China and the updated facts of the mental health of the Chinese rural older population. First, it looks back at China's history of urbanization and systematically reviews the country's policies on urbanization, based on which the definitions and typologies of China's urbanization are made. It is revealed that China's urbanization features massive rural-to-urban migration while loosening control over rural land use, mainly represented by social identity transition in individual life courses, family living-arrangement changes, and community environment restructuring. As such, in the second part, the social determinants of Chinese rural older people's mental health are reviewed accordingly. Thirdly, risk factors and consequences of mental health problems in older adults are systematically reviewed, revealing the policy direction and significance of dealing with the depression of the older population in China. Finally, the mental health situation of the Chinese rural older population, including depression, is reported, based on the findings of the local and national mental health surveys conducted between the 1990s and the 2010s.

References

Aboderin, I. (2004). Modernisation and aging theory revisited: Current explanations of recent developing world and historical Western shifts in material family support for older people. *Aging and Society, 24*(1), 29–50. doi:10.1017/S0144686X03001521

Alexopoulos, G. S. (2005). Depression in the elderly. *The Lancet, 365*(9475), 1961–1970. doi:10.1016/S0140-6736(05)66665-2

Allen, J., Balfour, R., Bell, R., & Marmot, M. (2014). Social determinants of mental health. *International Review of Psychiatry, 26*(4), 392–407. doi:10.3109/09540261.2014.928270

American Psychiatric Association. (2013). *Diagnostic and Statistical Manual of Mental Disorders.* Arlington: American Psychiatric Publishing.

Anda, R. F., Whitfield, C. L., Felitti, V. J., Chapman, D., Edwards, V. J., Dube, S. R., & Williamson, D. F. (2002). Adverse childhood experiences, alcoholic parents, and later risk of alcoholism and depression. *Psychiatric Services, 53*(8), 1001–1009. doi:10.1176/appi.ps.53.8.1001

Araya, R., Dunstan, F., Playle, R., Thomas, H., Palmer, S., & Lewis, G. (2006). Perceptions of social capital and the built environment and mental health. *Social Science & Medicine, 62*(12), 3072–3083. doi:10.1016/j.socscimed.2005.11.037

Axinn, W., Duncan, G. J., & Thornton, A. (1997). The effects of parents' income, wealth, and attitudes on children's completed schooling and self-esteem. In G. J. Duncan & J. Brooks-Gunn (Eds.), *Consequences of Growing Up Poor* (pp. 518–540). New York: Russell Sage.

Baldock, C. V. (2000). Migrants and their parents caregiving from a distance. *Journal of Family Issues, 21*(2), 205–224. doi:10.1177/019251300021002004

Beard, V. A., & Kunharibowo, Y. (2001). Living arrangements and support relationships among elderly Indonesians: Case studies from Java and Sumatra. *International Journal of Population Geography, 7*(1), 17–33. doi:10.1002/ijpg.202

Bian, F., Logan, J., & Bian, Y. (1998). Intergenerational relations in urban China: Proximity, contact, and help to parents. *Demography, 35*(1), 115–124. doi:10.2307/3004031

Black, C., & Ford-Gilboe, M. (2004). Adolescent mothers: Resilience, family health work and health-promoting practices. *Journal of Advanced Nursing, 48*(4), 351–360. doi:10.1111/j.1365-2648.2004.03204.x

Bradley, R. H., & Corwyn, R. F. (2002). Socioeconomic status and child development. *Annual Review of Psychology, 53*(1), 371–399. doi:10.1146/annurev.psych.53.100901.135233

Brady, D. (2004). Reconsidering the divergence between elderly, child, and overall poverty. *Research on Aging, 26*(5), 487–510. doi:10.1177/0164027504266587

Brown, A. S., & Susser, E. S. (2008). Prenatal nutritional deficiency and risk of adult schizophrenia. *Schizophrenia Bulletin, 34*(6), 1054–1063. doi:10.1016/j.socscimed.2009.01.027

Brown, S. L., Bulanda, J. R., & Lee, G. R. (2005). The significance of nonmarital cohabitation: Marital status and mental health benefits among middle-aged and older adults. *The Journals of Gerontology Series B: Psychological Sciences and Social Sciences, 60*(1), S21–S29. doi:10.1093/geronb/60.1.S21

Butterworth, P., Gill, S. C., Rodgers, B., Anstey, K. J., Villamil, E., & Melzer, D. (2006). Retirement and mental health: Analysis of the Australian national survey of mental health and well-being. *Social Science & Medicine, 62*(5), 1179–1191.

Chen, H., Hu, B., & Chen, X. (2004). Epidemiological survey on mental illness in Jiangxi in 2002. *Chinese Journal of Psychiatry, 37*(3), 172–175.

Chen, J., Chen, S., & Landry, P. F. (2013). Migration, environmental hazards, and health outcomes in China. *Social Science & Medicine, 80*, 85–95.

Chen, R., Wei, L., Hu, Z., Qin, X., Copeland, J. R., & Hemingway, H. (2005). Depression in older people in rural China. *Archives of Internal Medicine, 165*(17), 2019. doi:10.1001/archinte.165.17.2019.

Cherlin, A. J., Chase-Lansdale, P. L., & McRae, C. (1998). Effects of parental divorce on mental health throughout the life course. *American Sociological Review, 63*(2), 239–249.

Christakis, N. A., & Allison, P. D. (2006). Mortality after the hospitalization of a spouse. *New England Journal of Medicine, 354*(7), 719–730. doi:doi:10.1056/NEJMsa050196

Cohen, B. (2004). Urban growth in developing countries: A review of current trends and a caution regarding existing forecasts. *World Development, 32*(1), 23–51.

Cohen, B. (2006). Urbanization in developing countries: Current trends, future projections, and key challenges for sustainability. *Technology in Society, 28*(1), 63–80.

Collishaw, S., Pickles, A., Messer, J., Rutter, M., Shearer, C., & Maughan, B. (2007). Resilience to adult psychopathology following childhood maltreatment: Evidence from a community sample. *Child Abuse & Neglect, 31*(3), 211–229. doi:10.1016/j.chiabu.2007.02.004

Cornwell, E. Y., & Waite, L. J. (2009). Social disconnectedness, perceived isolation, and health among older adults. *Journal of Health and Social Behavior, 50*(1), 31–48. doi: 10.1177/002214650905000103

Couch, C., Leontidou, L., & Petschel-Held, G. (2007). *Urban Sprawl in Europe*. Hoboken, NJ: Wiley.

Cutrona, C. E., Wallace, G., & Wesner, K. A. (2006). Neighborhood characteristics and depression an examination of stress processes. *Current Directions in Psychological Science, 15*(4), 188–192. doi:10.1111/j.1467-8721.2006.00433.x

Dantzer, R., O'Connor, J. C., Freund, G. G., Johnson, R. W., & Kelley, K. W. (2008). From inflammation to sickness and depression: When the immune system subjugates the brain. *Nature Reviews Neuroscience, 9*(1), 46–56. doi:10.1038/nrn2297

Demuth, S., & Brown, S. L. (2004). Family structure, family processes, and adolescent delinquency: The significance of parental absence versus parental gender. *Journal of Research in Crime and Delinquency, 41*(1), 58–81. doi:10.1177/0022427803256236

Du, P., Ding, Z., Li, Q., & Gui, J. (2004). The impact of out labor migration on the elderly stayers in rural areas. *Population Research, 28*(6), 44–52.

Du, Y., Park, A., & Wang, S. (2005). Migration and rural poverty in China. *Journal of Comparative Economics, 33*(4), 688–709. doi:10.1016/j.jce.2005.09.001

Edwards, V. J., Holden, G. W., Felitti, V. J., & Anda, R. F. (2003). Relationship between multiple forms of childhood maltreatment and adult mental health in community respondents: Results from the adverse childhood experiences study. *American Journal of Psychiatry, 160*(8), 1453–1460. doi:10.1176/appi. ajp.160.8.1453

Egede, L. E. (2004). Diabetes, major depression, and functional disability among US adults. *Diabetes Care, 27*(2), 421–428. doi:10.2337/diacare.27.2.421

Evans, G. (2003). The built environment and mental health. *Journal of Urban Health, 80*(4), 536–555. doi:10.1093/jurban/jtg063

Fergusson, D. M., & Horwood, L. J. (2003). Resilience to childhood adversity: Results of a 21-year study. In S. S. Luthar (Ed.), *Resilience and Vulnerability: Adaptation in the Context of Childhood Adversities* (pp. 130–155). Cambridge: Cambridge University Press.

Ferrari, A. J., Charlson, F. J., Norman, R. E., Patten, S. B., Freedman, G., Murray, C. J., ... Whiteford, H. A. (2013). Burden of depressive disorders by country, sex, age, and year: Findings from the global burden of disease study 2010. *PLoS Medicine, 10*(11), e1001547. doi:10.1371/journal.pmed.1001547

Fiori, K. L., Antonucci, T. C., & Cortina, K. S. (2006). Social network typologies and mental health among older adults. *The Journals of Gerontology Series B: Psychological Sciences and Social Sciences, 61*(1), P25–P32.

Förster, M. F., & Mira D'Ercole, M. (2005). Income distribution and poverty in OECD countries in the second half of the 1990s, OECD Social, Employment and Migration Working Papers No. 22. Organisation for Economic Co-operation and Development, Paris, France.

Frankenberg, E., Chan, A., & Ofstedal, M. B. (2002). Stability and change in living arrangements in Indonesia, Singapore, and Taiwan, 1993–99. *Population Studies, 56*(2), 201–213. doi:10.1080/00324720215928

Fraser, C., Jackson, H., Judd, F., Komiti, A., Robins, G., Murray, G., ... Hodgins, G. (2005). Changing places: The impact of rural restructuring on mental health in Australia. *Health & Place, 11*(2), 157–171.

Frumkin, H., Frank, L., & Jackson, R. J. (2004). *Urban Sprawl and Public Health: Designing, Planning, and Building for Healthy Communities.* Washington, DC: Island Press.

Fryers, T., & Brugha, T. (2013). Childhood determinants of adult psychiatric disorder. *Clinical Practice and Epidemiology in Mental Health, 9*, 1. doi:10.2174/1745017901309010001

Fryers, T., Melzer, D., & Jenkins, R. (2003). Social inequalities and the common mental disorders. *Social Psychiatry and Psychiatric Epidemiology, 38*(5), 229–237. doi:10.1007/s00127-003-0627-2

Fujisawa, D., Miyashita, M., Nakajima, S., Ito, M., Kato, M., & Kim, Y. (2010). Prevalence and determinants of complicated grief in general population. *Journal of Affective Disorders, 127*(1), 352–358. doi:10.1016/j.jad.2010.06.008

Fultz, N. H., Jenkins, K. R., Østbye, T., Taylor, D. H., Kabeto, M. U., & Langa, K. M. (2005). The impact of own and spouse's urinary incontinence on depressive symptoms. *Social Science & Medicine, 60*(11), 2537–2548. doi:10.1016/j.socscimed.2004.11.019

Gapen, M., Cross, D., Ortigo, K., Graham, A., Johnson, E., Evces, M., ... Bradley, B. (2011). Perceived neighborhood disorder, community cohesion, and PTSD symptoms among low-income African Americans in an urban health setting.

American Journal of Orthopsychiatry, 81(1), 31–37. doi:10.1111/j.1939-0025. 2010.01069.x

Girardet, H. (1996). *The Gaia Atlas of Cities: New Directions for Sustainable Urban Living.* UN-HABITAT, London, United Kingdom.

Gong, P., Liang, S., Carlton, E. J., Jiang, Q., Wu, J., Wang, L., & Remais, J. V. (2012). Urbanisation and health in China. *The Lancet, 379*(9818), 843–852. doi:10.1016/S0140-6736(11)61878-3

Gornick, J. C., Munzi, T., Sierminska, E., & Smeeding, T. M. (2009). Income, assets, and poverty: Older women in comparative perspective. *Journal of Women, Politics & Policy, 30*(2–3), 272–300. doi:10.1080/15544770902901791

Green, J. G., McLaughlin, K. A., Berglund, P. A., Gruber, M. J., Sampson, N. A., Zaslavsky, A. M., & Kessler, R. C. (2010). Childhood adversities and adult psychiatric disorders in the national comorbidity survey replication I: Associations with first onset of DSM-IV disorders. *Archives of General Psychiatry, 67*(2), 113–123. doi:10.1001/archgenpsychiatry.2009.186

Guo, M., Aranda, M. P., & Silverstein, M. (2009). The impact of out-migration on the inter-generational support and psychological wellbeing of older adults in rural China. *Aging and Society, 29*(7), 1085.

Guo, X. (2001). Land expropriation and rural conflicts in China. *The China Quarterly, 166*, 422–439.

Ha, J. H. (2008). Changes in support from confidants, children, and friends following widowhood. *Journal of Marriage and Family, 70*(2), 306–318. doi:10.1111/j.1741-3737.2008.00483.x

Hank, K. (2007). Proximity and contacts between older parents and their children: A European comparison. *Journal of Marriage and Family, 69*(1), 157–173. doi:10.1111/j.1741-3737.2006.00351.x

Harpham, T., & Molyneux, C. (2001). Urban health in developing countries: A review. *Progress in Development Studies, 1*(2), 113–137.

Hellstrom, K., Lindmark, B., Wahlberg, B., & Fugl-Meyer, A. R. (2003). Self-efficacy in relation to impairments and activities of daily living disability in elderly patients with stroke: A prospective investigation. *Journal of Rehabilitation Medicine, 35*(5), 202–207. doi:10.1080/16501970310000836

Hill, T. D., Ross, C. E., & Angel, R. J. (2005). Neighborhood disorder, psychophysiological distress, and health. *Journal of Health and Social Behavior, 46*(2), 170–186. doi:10.1177/002214650504600204

Hooten, W. M., Shi, Y., Gazelka, H. M., & Warner, D. O. (2011). The effects of depression and smoking on pain severity and opioid use in patients with chronic pain. *PAIN, 152*(1), 223–229. doi:10.1016/j.pain.2010.10.045

Horwitz, A. V., & White, H. R. (1998). The relationship of cohabitation and mental health: A study of a young adult cohort. *Journal of Marriage and the Family, 60*(2), 505–514. doi:10.2307/353865

Hu, J., Li, Z., & Chen, Y. (2002). Epidemiological survey on mental illness in Zhongshan, Guangdong. *Chinese Journal of Psychiatry, 28*(6), 456–458.

Huang, Y. (2008). A review of the epidemiological studies on mental disorders in China. *China Preventive Medicine, 9*(5), 445–446.

Huang, Y., Wang, Y., Wang, H., Liu, Z., Yu, X., Yan, J., … Lu, J. (2019). Prevalence of mental disorders in China: A cross-sectional epidemiological study. *The Lancet Psychiatry, 6*(3), 211–224.

Hubicka, B., Källmén, H., Hiltunen, A., & Bergman, H. (2010). Personality traits and mental health of severe drunk drivers in Sweden. *Social Psychiatry and Psychiatric Epidemiology, 45*(7), 723–731. doi:10.1007/s00127-009-0111-8

Ilbery, B. (2014). *The Geography of Rural Change*: London: Routledge.

Imai, K. S., Gaiha, R., Ali, A., & Kaicker, N. (2014). Remittances, growth and poverty: New evidence from Asian countries. *Journal of Policy Modeling, 36*(3), 524–538. doi:10.1016/j.jpolmod.2014.01.009

Jenkins, R., Bhugra, D., Bebbington, P., Brugha, T., Farrell, M., Coid, J., … Meltzer, H. (2008). Debt, income and mental disorder in the general population. *Psychological medicine, 38*(10), 1485–1493. doi:10.1017/S0033291707002516

Jones, P. B., Rantakallio, P., Hartikainen, A.-L., Isohanni, M., & Sipila, P. (1998). Schizophrenia as a long-term outcome of pregnancy, delivery, and perinatal complications: A 28-year follow-up of the 1966 north Finland general population birth cohort. *American Journal of Psychiatry, 155*(3), 355–364. doi:10.1176/ajp.155.3.355

Kasen, S., Cohen, P., Skodol, A. E., Johnson, J. G., Smailes, E., & Brook, J. S. (2001). Childhood depression and adult personality disorder: Alternative pathways of continuity. *Archives of General Psychiatry, 58*(3), 231–236. doi:10.1001/archpsyc.58.3.231.

Katz, R. (2009). Intergenerational family relations and subjective well-being in old age: A cross-national study. *European Journal of Aging, 6*(2), 79–90. doi:10.1007/s10433-009-0113-0

Kelly, Y., Sacker, A., Del Bono, E., Francesconi, M., & Marmot, M. (2011). What role for the home learning environment and parenting in reducing the socioeconomic gradient in child development? Findings from the Millennium Cohort Study. *Archives of Disease in Childhood, 96*(9), 832–837. doi:10.1136/adc.2010.195917

Kendler, K. S., Walters, E. E., Neale, M. C., Kessler, R. C., Heath, A. C., & Eaves, L. J. (1995). The structure of the genetic and environmental risk factors for six major psychiatric disorders in women: Phobia, generalized anxiety disorder, panic disorder, bulimia, major depression, and alcoholism. *Archives of General Psychiatry, 52*(5), 374–383. doi:10.1001/archpsyc.1995.03950170048007.

Kersting, A., Brähler, E., Glaesmer, H., & Wagner, B. (2011). Prevalence of complicated grief in a representative population-based sample. *Journal of Affective Disorders, 131*(1), 339–343. doi:10.1016/j.jad.2010.11.032

Kessler, R. C., Davis, C. G., & Kendler, K. S. (1997). Childhood adversity and adult psychiatric disorder in the US National Comorbidity Survey. *Psychological Medicine, 27*(5), 1101–1119. doi:10.1017/S0033291797005588

Kreager, P. (2006). Migration, social structure and old-age support networks: A comparison of three Indonesian communities. *Aging and Society, 26*(1), 37–60. doi:10.1017/S0144686X05004411

Kuhn, R. S. (2005). A longitudinal analysis of health and mortality in a migrant-sending region of Bangladesh. In S. Jatrana, M. Toyota, & B. S. A. Yeoh (Eds.), *Migration and Health in Asia* (pp. 177). New York: Routledge.

Kulminski, A., Yashin, A., Ukraintseva, S., Akushevich, I., Arbeev, K., Land, K., & Manton, K. (2006). Accumulation of health disorders as a systemic measure of aging: Findings from the NLTCS data. *Mechanisms of Aging and Development, 127*(11), 840–848. doi:10.1016/j.mad.2006.08.005

Lehtinen, V., Sohlman, B., & Kovess-Masfety, V. (2005). Level of positive mental health in the European Union: Results from the Eurobarometer 2002 survey. *Clinical Practice and Epidemiology in Mental Health, 1*(1), 9. doi:10.1186/1745-0179-1-9

Li, K., Cui, Z., & Cui, L. (2007). Epidemiological survey on the mental illness in Hebei Province. *Chinese Journal of Psychiatry, 40*(1), 36–40.

Liao, C., & Heaton, T. B. (1992). Divorce trends and differentials in China. *Journal of Comparative Family Studies*, 413–429.

Lin, Y., Zhang, X., Zhao, H., Chen, P., Zhuang, X., Zhao, D., ... Luo, K. (1998). Epidemiological survey on mental illness in Shantou. *Chinese Journal of Psychiatry, 31*(2), 127.

Louis, V. V., & Zhao, S. (2002). Effects of family structure, family SES, and adulthood experiences on life satisfaction. *Journal of Family Issues, 23*(8), 986–1005. doi:10.1177/019251302237300

Lu, Y. (2012). Household migration, social support, and psychosocial health: The perspective from migrant-sending areas. *Social Science & Medicine, 74*(2), 135–142. doi:10.1016/j.socscimed.2011.10.020

Lund, C., Breen, A., Flisher, A. J., Kakuma, R., Corrigall, J., Joska, J. A., ... Patel, V. (2010). Poverty and common mental disorders in low and middle income countries: A systematic review. *Social Science & Medicine, 71*(3), 517–528. doi:10.1016/j.socscimed.2010.04.027

Luo, Y., & Waite, L. J. (2005). The impact of childhood and adult SES on physical, mental, and cognitive well-being in later life. *The Journals of Gerontology Series B: Psychological Sciences and Social Sciences, 60*(2), S93–S101.

Marsella, A. J. (1998). Urbanization, mental health, and social deviancy: A review of issues and research. *American Psychologist, 53*(6), 624. doi:10.1037/0003-066X.53.6.624

Martinez, C., Rietbrock, S., Wise, L., Ashby, D., Chick, J., Moseley, J., ... Gunnell, D. (2005). Antidepressant treatment and the risk of fatal and non-fatal self harm in first episode depression: Nested case-control study. *BMJ, 330*(7488), 389. doi:10.1136/bmj.330.7488.389

Mickus, M., Colenda, C. C., & Hogan, A. J. (2000). Knowledge of mental health benefits and preferences for type of mental health providers among the general public. *Psychiatric Services, 51*(2), 199–202. doi:10.1176/appi.ps.51.2.199

Mitnitski, A., & Rockwood, K. (2006). Decrease in the relative heterogeneity of health with age: A cross-national comparison. *Mechanisms of Aging and Development, 127*(1), 70–72. doi:10.1016/j.mad.2005.09.007

Mokyr, J. (1995). Urbanization, technological progress, and economic history. In *Urban Agglomeration and Economic Growth* (pp. 3–37). New York: Springer.

Moon, T. W., & Hur, W.-M. (2011). Emotional intelligence, emotional exhaustion, and job performance. *Social Behavior and Personality: An International Journal, 39*(8), 1087–1096. doi:10.2224/sbp.2011.39.8.1087

Morokoff, P. J., Redding, C. A., Harlow, L. L., Cho, S., Rossi, J. S., Meier, K. S., … Brown-Peterside, P. (2009). Associations of sexual victimization, depression, and sexual assertiveness with unprotected sex: A test of the multifaceted model of HIV risk across gender. *Journal of Applied Biobehavioral Research, 14*(1), 30–54. doi:10.1111/j.1751-9861.2009.00039.x

Musselman, D. L., Evans, D. L., & Nemeroff, C. B. (1998). The relationship of depression to cardiovascular disease: Epidemiology, biology, and treatment. *Archives of General Psychiatry, 55*(7), 580–592. doi:10.1001/archpsyc.55. 7.580.

Ng, C. H. (1997). The stigma of mental illness in Asian cultures. *Australian and New Zealand Journal of Psychiatry, 31*(3), 382–390. doi:10.3109/00048679709073848

Northridge, M., Sclar, E., & Biswas, P. (2003). Sorting out the connections between the built environment and health: A conceptual framework for navigating pathways and planning healthy cities. *Journal of Urban Health, 80*(4), 556–568. doi:10.1093/jurban/jtg064

Nunes, E. V., & Levin, F. R. (2004). Treatment of depression in patients with alcohol or other drug dependence: A meta-analysis. *JAMA, 291*(15), 1887–1896. doi:10.1001/jama.291.15.1887.

Obasaju, M. A., Palin, F. L., Jacobs, C., Anderson, P., & Kaslow, N. J. (2009). Won't you be my neighbor? Using an ecological approach to examine the impact of community on revictimization. *Journal of Interpersonal Violence, 24*(1), 38–53. doi:10.1177/0886260508314933

Painter, R. C., De Rooij, S. R., Bossuyt, P. M., Osmond, C., Barker, D. J., Bleker, O. P., & Roseboom, T. J. (2006). A possible link between prenatal exposure to famine and breast cancer: A preliminary study. *American Journal of Human Biology, 18*(6), 853–856. doi:10.1002/ajhb.20564

Painter, R. C., Roseboom, T. J., & Bleker, O. P. (2005). Prenatal exposure to the Dutch famine and disease in later life: An overview. *Reproductive Toxicology, 20*(3), 345–352. doi:10.1016/j.reprotox.2005.04.005

Patel, V., & Kleinman, A. (2003). Poverty and common mental disorders in developing countries. *Bulletin of the World Health Organization, 81*(8), 609–615. doi:10.1590/S0042-96862003000800011

Patel, V., & Prince, M. (2001). Aging and mental health in a developing country: Who cares? Qualitative studies from Goa, India. *Psychological Medicine, 31*(1), 29–38.

Patel, V., Lund, C., Hatherill, S., Plagerson, S., Corrigall, J., Funk, M., & Flisher, A. J. (2010). Mental disorders: Equity and social determinants. In E. Blas & A. S. Kurup (Eds.), *Equity, Social Determinants and Public Health Programmes* (pp. 115–134). Geneva, Switzerland: World Health Organization.

Penninx, B. W., Leveille, S., Ferrucci, L., Van Eijk, J., & Guralnik, J. M. (1999). Exploring the effect of depression on physical disability: Longitudinal evidence from the established populations for epidemiologic studies of the elderly. *American Journal of Public Health, 89*(9), 1346–1352. doi:10.2105/ AJPH.89.9.1346

Phillips, M. R., Zhang, J., Shi, Q., Song, Z., Ding, Z., Pang, S., … Wang, Z. (2009). Prevalence, treatment, and associated disability of mental disorders in four provinces in China during 2001–05: An epidemiological survey. *The Lancet, 373*(9680), 2041–2053. doi:10.1016/S0140-6736(09)60660-7

Pinquart, M., & Sörensen, S. (2003). Differences between caregivers and noncaregivers in psychological health and physical health: A meta-analysis. *Psychology and Aging, 18*(2), 250. doi:10.1037/0882-7974.18.2.250

Pinquart, M., & Sörensen, S. (2000). Influences of socioeconomic status, social network, and competence on subjective well-being in later life: A meta-analysis. *Psychology and Aging, 15*(2), 187. doi:10.1037/0882-7974.15.2.187

Reddy, M. (2010). Depression: The disorder and the burden. *Indian Journal of Psychological Medicine, 32*(1), 1. doi:10.4103/0253-7176.70510

Repetti, R. L., Taylor, S. E., & Seeman, T. E. (2002). Risky families: Family social environments and the mental and physical health of offspring. *Psychological Bulletin, 128*(2), 330. doi:10.1037/0033-2909.128.2.330

Robert, S. A. (1998). Community-level socioeconomic status effects on adult health. *Journal of Health and Social Behavior*, 18–37.

Roseboom, T., de Rooij, S., & Painter, R. (2006). The Dutch famine and its long-term consequences for adult health. *Early Human Development, 82*(8), 485–491. doi:10.1016/j.earlhumdev.2006.07.001

Ross, C. E., & Mirowsky, J. (2001). Neighborhood disadvantage, disorder, and health. *Journal of Health and Social Behavior, 42*(3), 258–276.

Sampson, R. J. (1991). Linking the micro-and macrolevel dimensions of community social organization. *Social Forces, 70*(1), 43–64. doi:10.1093/sf/70.1.43

Sander, J., & McCarty, C. (2005). Youth Depression in the Family Context: Familial Risk Factors and Models of Treatment. *Clinical Child and Family Psychology Review, 8*(3), 203–219. doi:10.1007/s10567-005-6666-3

Scarpaci, J. L. (2000). On the transformation of socialist cities. *Urban Geography, 21*(8), 659–669.

Serby, M., & Yu, M. (2003). Overview: Depression in the elderly. *The Mount Sinai Journal of Medicine, 70*(1), 38–44.

Shi, Q., Zhang, J., & Xu, F. (2005). Epidemiological survey on the mental illness of people aged 15 or above in Zhejiang Province. *Chinese Journal of Preventive Medcine, 39*(4), 229–236.

Shonkoff, J. P., Garner, A. S., Siegel, B. S., Dobbins, M. I., Earls, M. F., McGuinn, L., … Wood, D. L. (2012). The lifelong effects of early childhood adversity and toxic stress. *Pediatrics, 129*(1), e232–e246. doi:10.1542/peds.2011-2663

Siegel, M. J., Bradley, E. H., Gallo, W. T., & Kasl, S. V. (2004). The effect of spousal mental and physical health on husbands' and wives' depressive symptoms, among older adults longitudinal evidence from the health and retirement survey. *Journal of Aging and Health, 16*(3), 398–425. doi:10.1177/0898264304264208

Silver, A. (2014). Families across borders: The emotional impacts of migration on origin families. *International Migration, 52*(3), 194–220. doi:10.1111/j.1468-2435.2010.00672.x

Skogan, W. G. (1989). Communities, crime, and neighborhood organization. *Crime & Delinquency, 35*(3), 437–457. doi:10.1177/0011128789035003008

Smil, V. (1999). China's great famine: 40 years later. *BMJ: British Medical Journal, 319*(7225), 1619.

Smith, G. C. (1998). Residential separation and patterns of interaction between elderly parents and their adult children. *Progress in Human Geography, 22*(3), 368–384. doi:10.1191/030913298673626843

Song, S., Wang, W., & Hu, P. (2009). Famine, death, and madness: Schizophrenia in early adulthood after prenatal exposure to the Chinese great leap forward famine. *Social Science & Medicine, 68*(7), 1315–1321. doi:10.1016/j.socscimed.2009.01.027

Spataro, J., Mullen, P. E., Burgess, P. M., Wells, D. L., & Moss, S. A. (2004). Impact of child sexual abuse on mental health Prospective study in males and females. *The British Journal of Psychiatry, 184*(5), 416–421.

State Council of China. (2014). *China New Urbanization Planning (2014–2020)*. Retrieved from http://www.gov.cn/gongbao/content/2014/content_2644805.htm

Stice, E., & Shaw, H. (2004). Eating disorder prevention programs: A meta-analytic review. *Psychological Bulletin, 130*(2), 206. doi:10.1037/0033-2909.130.2.206

Sturm, R., & Cohen, D. A. (2004). Suburban sprawl and physical and mental health. *Public Health, 118*(7), 488–496.

Timberlake, M., & Kentor, J. (1983). Economic dependence, overurbanization, and economic growth: A study of less developed countries. *Sociological Quarterly, 24*(4), 489–507.

Tolan, P. H., Gorman-Smith, D., Huesmann, L. R., & Zelli, A. (1997). Assessment of family relationship characteristics: A measure to explain risk for antisocial behavior and depression among urban youth. *Psychological Assessment, 9*(3), 212. doi:10.1037/1040-3590.9.3.212

Topa, G., Moriano, J. A., Depolo, M., Alcover, C.-M., & Morales, J. F. (2009). Antecedents and consequences of retirement planning and decision-making: A meta-analysis and model. *Journal of Vocational Behavior, 75*(1), 38–55. doi:10.1016/j.jvb.2009.03.002

Turley, R., Saith, R., Bhan, N., Rehfuess, E., & Carter, B. (2013). *Slum Upgrading Strategies Involving Physical Environment and Infrastructure Interventions and Their Effects on Health and Socio-economic Outcomes*. The Cochrane Library. doi:10.1002/14651858.CD010067.pub2

United Nations. (1997). *Glossary of Environment Statistics*. Retrieved from New York: United Nations.

Vanderhorst, R. K., & McLaren, S. (2005). Social relationships as predictors of depression and suicidal ideation in older adults. *Aging & Mental Health, 9*(6), 517–525. doi:10.1080/13607860500193062

Wainwright, N., & Surtees, P. (2002). Childhood adversity, gender and depression over the life-course. *Journal of Affective Disorders, 72*(1), 33–44. doi:10.1016/S0165-0327(01)00420-7

Wang, C. (2001). Social identity of the new generation of rural hobo and merger of urban and rural. *Sociological Research, 3*, 63–76.

Wang, F.-L. (2005). *Organizing through Division and Exclusion: China's Hukou System*. Stanford, CA: Stanford University Press.

Wang, J., & Zhao, X. (2012). Family functioning and social support for older patients with depression in an urban area of Shanghai, China. *Archives of Gerontology and Geriatrics, 55*(3), 574–579. doi:10.1016/j.archger.2012.06.011

Weich, S., Blanchard, M., Prince, M., Burton, E., Erens, B., & Sproston, K. (2002). Mental health and the built environment: Cross-sectional survey of individual and contextual risk factors for depression. *The British Journal of Psychiatry, 180*(5), 428–433. doi:10.1192/bjp.180.5.428

Werner, E. E., & Smith, R. S. (2001). *Journeys from Childhood to Midlife: Risk, Resilience, and Recovery.* Ithaca, NY: Cornell University Press.

World Health Organization. (2012). *Mental Health Atlas-2011.* Retrieved from Geneva, Switzerland: World Health Organization.

World Health Organization, & Calouste Gulbenkian Foundation. (2014). *Social Determinants of Mental Health.* Retrieved from Geneva, Switzerland: World Health Organization.

Wright, P. A., & Kloos, B. (2007). Housing environment and mental health outcomes: A levels of analysis perspective. *Journal of Environmental Psychology, 27*(1), 79–89. doi:10.1016/j.jenvp.2006.12.001

Yang, C., & Wu, C. (1996). *Ten-Year Reform of Land Use System in China.* Dadi Publishing House of China, Beijing.

Yang, F., & Lou, V. W. (2016). Childhood adversities, urbanisation and depressive symptoms among middle-aged and older adults: Evidence from a national survey in China. *Aging & Society, 36*(5), 1031–1051.

Yang, L. (2011). A study on the size of China's poor older population. *Population Journal, 4*, 37–45.

Yang, L. H., & Kleinman, A. (2008). 'Face'and the embodiment of stigma in China: The cases of schizophrenia and AIDS. *Social Science & Medicine, 67*(3), 398–408. doi:10.1016/j.socscimed.2008.03.011

Yashin, A. I., Ukraintseva, S. V., Boiko, S. I., & Arbeev, K. G. (2002). Individual aging and mortality rate: How are they related? *Biodemography and Social Biology, 49*(3–4), 206–217. doi:10.1080/19485565.2002.9989059

Ye, M., & Chen, Y. (2014). The influence of domestic living arrangement and neighborhood identity on mental health among urban Chinese elders. *Aging & Mental Health, 18*(1), 40–50. doi:10.1080/13607863.2013.837142

Zhan, H. J. (2004). Willingness and expectations: Intergenerational differences in attitudes toward filial responsibility in China. *Marriage & Family Review, 36*(1–2), 175–200. doi:10.1300/J002v36n01_08

Zhang, L. (2008). Conceptualizing China's urbanization under reforms. *Habitat International, 32*(4), 452–470. doi:10.1016/j.habitatint.2008.01.001

Zhang, L., Wang, H., Wang, L., & Hsiao, W. (2006). Social capital and farmer's willingness-to-join a newly established community-based health insurance in rural China. Health Policy, 76(2), 233–242. doi:10.1016/j.healthpol.2005.06.001

Zhao, Z., Huang, Y., & Li, J. (2009). Epidemiological survey on mental illness of permanent residents in Guangzhou. *Chinese Journal of Psychiatry, 35*(9), 530–534.

Zhou, Y., & Ma, L. J. (2003). China's urbanization levels: Reconstructing a baseline from the fifth population census. *The China Quarterly, 173*, 176–196. doi:10.1017/S000944390300010X

3 Theoretical framework and data sources

3.1 Depression of older adults in the perspective of the life course

Three theories have frequently been applied in discussing the life-course context for the mental health of an aging population. The first is the life-course theory or life-course perspective. It holds that a society is characterized by a structured set of positions to be occupied by individuals throughout their interconnected life stages. Also, society is embedded with a set of mechanisms that enforce constraints or allow opportunities for mobility through the structured field (Marshall, 2009). According to Elder (1998), there are five principles for the life-course theory, including (1) human development and aging are lifelong process consisting of interconnected stages; (2) historical times and places one experiences throughout one's lifetime are associated with one's life course; (3) the antecedents and consequences of life transitions and events vary according to their timing in one's life; (4) the effects of social and historical transformations on the life course are imposed through the network of interconnected individual lives; and (5) one constructs his or her own life course through the choices and actions taken within certain social circumstances.

The second is the cumulative advantage/disadvantage theory. Originally being a framework of analyzing development in scientific careers in the 1970s, the cumulative theory later received widespread attention in the social science literature on inequalities in wealth distribution, social mobility, education, race, and human development (DiPrete & Eirich, 2006). It mainly depicts a diverged cohort trajectory in the life course and the process of forming the Matthew effect. It proposes that the disadvantage of one individual or group compared with another accumulates over time, and the disadvantage in question is typically social mainstream resources or reward in the social stratification process, such as career hierarchy, income, wealth, physical health, and cognitive development (Dannefer, 2003).

DOI: 10.4324/9781003248767-3

The third is the developmental adaptation model (DAM). The DAM derived from the Georgia Adaptation Model (GAM) (Poon et al., 1992), a useful framework for the study of longevity and adaptation in later life. Making a further step, DAM included distal experiences of older adults. The general assumption in the DAM is that personal resources and experiential factors optimize adaptation over the life span (Fry & Debats, 2006). This model integrates distal influences, resources, behavioral skills, and developmental outcomes. Intervening variables, individual, social and economic resources, proximal life events, and behavioral coping skills represent the contribution of adaptation processes to positive developmental adaptation outcomes. Moreover, distal life events, including stressors and past achievements, signify the influences of distal experiences and events. Finally, the developmental outcomes reflect fundamental quality-of-life characteristics, which can be represented by functional capacity, self-rated health, cognitive capacity, mental health, economic cost and burden, psychological wellbeing, longevity, among many others (Martin & Martin, 2002).

In China's context, the DAM is a suitable framework for analyzing the individual-level effects of urbanization on the depression of the older population. On the one hand, it takes into account the distal experiences. For the current older Chinese, their childhood period was spent in a society that featured dire poverty and communist fever, which can have lifelong impacts on their mental wellbeing. On the other hand, it includes the proximal experiences and personal resources that optimize adaptation over the life span. China's urbanization initiated in the late 1970s and early 1980s and accelerated only in the late 1990s, which is a relatively proximal experience for older people in China. Moreover, the urbanization process involves migration and identity transformation, which is closely related to the change of personal economic and social resources. Therefore, the DAM can effectively connect the different life stages of the current older population in China, as well as disentangle the mental health effects of the dynamics within urbanization.

3.2 Depression of older people and family living arrangements

The attachment theory, the stress-buffering model, and the stress process model have been frequently applied to framing the association between household environment and depression or other aspects of mental health of older populations. Based on the proposition that deficits in security or support in family relationships and avoidant personal traits are associated with poorer mental health, the attachment theory conceptualizes four attachment styles of adult people, including secure, dismissing-avoidant, preoccupied-ambivalent, and fearful-avoidant (Bartholomew & Horowitz, 1991). Applying this typology to the older population, it is found that secure older people, namely those having adequate family attachment but low avoidance, are featured with more self-esteem and help-seeking skills, which facilitate the stress-coping process. The dismissing-avoidant elderly, featuring low family attachment needs but high avoidance, are more likely to be self-reliant. The preoccupied-ambivalent elderly, on the contrary, would have high family attachment needs but low avoidance. They often seek excessive family care. Finally, the fearful-avoidant older people have high family attachment needs and avoidance, and they may withdraw from family relations due to the fear of rejection. Under this framework, the mental health of older people is a result of the interaction between the perceived availability of family support and the level of avoidance in older people's characters (Poon, 2013).

Another theoretical perspective comes from the stress-buffering model. This model focuses on the functional aspects of family relations (e.g., perceived family support) and posits that family supports are associated with mental wellbeing only for persons with stress (Raffaelli et al., 2013). It hypothesizes that the process of responding to stressful life events is harmful to mental health, which can be buffered by the perceived availability of family support or received family support. On the one hand, the perceived availability of family support can ameliorate one's appraisal of a situation when a stressful life event happens, which prevents a cascade of ensuing negative behavioral and emotional responses (Acevedo, Ellison, & Xu, 2014). On the other hand, perceived or received family support may either reduce the negative emotional reaction to a stressful event or dampen the physiologic/behavioral responses to stress (Kawachi & Berkman, 2001).

As with the stress process model, it represents the mainstream theoretical perspective in identifying potentially modifiable social contingencies in mental health (Turner, 2010). Within the context of socioeconomic status, the model incorporates multiple resources and stressors to predict mental health outcomes. At the family level, it mainly pays attention to how family socioeconomic status and family type affect one's stress exposure as well as the availability of social and personal resources used to cope with it. The model on the one hand recognizes the mediating role of social and personal resources between the stressors (e.g., recent stressful events, lifetime traumas, and discrimination stress) and mental health outcomes; while on the other hand, it also notes the moderating effects of the two levels of resources. According to the stress process model, social resources refer to social support and social network, and personal resources refer to self-esteem, sense of control, emotional resilience, and mattering (Pearlin, Menaghan, Lieberman, & Mullan, 1981).

In the context of China, the stress-buffering model is a suitable framework in analyzing the household-level effects of urbanization on the mental health of the mature and older population. The reasons are two-fold. First, it pays adequate attention to family characteristics and family-level risk factors for mental health. The most obvious influence of urbanization on a Chinese family is the change of family living arrangements. Currently, there are over 200 million rural migrant workers in the urban sector, and more than 10 million rural people are adding to the population each year (National Bureau of Statistics of China, 2015). The overwhelming majority of them do not migrate with family members but leave the non-working-age family members, namely the old and the young children, behind in rural hometown. Separation from close relatives may have significant effects on the left-behind elderly (Biao, 2007). Moreover, many of these people have to shoulder grandparenting responsibilities, which can be another significant life stressor (Zeng & Xie, 2014). Second, it stresses the role of social and personal resources in coping with life stressors. For the aging population in rural China, the living-arrangement change resulting from urbanization has a significant impact on the resources available for them to cope with life stressors. For instance, their income may increase due to the remittance from the family members working in the city; while at the same time, they can suffer from loneliness and helplessness due to the absence of adult children.

3.3 Depression of older adults and community environment

The existing literature on the association between community environment and mental health is mainly guided by three theories, namely social cognitive theory, fundamental causes theory, and social network theory. Social cognitive theory was initially developed to understand how human social behaviors are formed (Bandura, 2001). In the health literature, it is frequently applied to analyze health behaviors. According to Armitage and Conner (2000), health behaviors are decided by self-efficacy and outcome expectancies. Self-efficacy is more about a positive personal trait, which decides an individual's confidence and determination to achieve behavior change through overcoming obstacles such as stressful life events and financial strain. On the other hand, outcome expectancies are more affected by social environment, including community environment. That is, outcome expectancies are associated with the perception that behavioral outcome is a result of the environment. As noted by Bandura (2012), personal agency develops, adapts, and changes within a broad network of socio-structural influences, meaning that socio-demographic characteristics, such as quality of neighborhood, can significantly affect one's behavior, and in turn one's health.

As with the fundamental causes theory, it focuses on the association between community socioeconomic status and mental health disparities. The theory proposes that community socioeconomic status is the fundamental cause of people's mental health (Phelan, Link, & Tehranifar, 2010). The reasons are two-fold. First, high community socioeconomic status means access to more resources that prevent people from experiencing mental problems. These resources include community health and education services, facilities, and economic development (Phelan, Link, Diez-Roux, Kawachi, & Levin, 2004). Second, community socioeconomic status can shape exposure to and experience of most risk factors for mental health. Communities with high socioeconomic positions are usually well designed, which prevents them coming into contact with overcrowding, air pollution, high crime rates, and other environment and social risks (Frishman, 2012).

A number of psychological pathways linking community environment and mental wellbeing have been proposed under the social network theory. The first is in relation to information. That is, the community environment may affect the receipt of relevant information on positive behaviors that help to avoid negative events and facilitate stress coping (Cohen, 2004). Second, the community environment may affect mental health through shaping identity and self-esteem. That is, the social networks in the community can be a source of positive affect, which affects motivation, controls neuroendocrine response, and enhances self-control (Kawachi & Berkman, 2001). The third pathway is social influence, which disentangles how social norms and peer group pressure influence individual health behaviors. Many studies have reported that people tend to refer to reference groups, namely those with similar attitudes and socioeconomic position on how to react and behave (Shields, Price, & Wooden, 2009). As such, social networks and acquaintanceship in community can affect people's health behavior and, in turn, mental health significantly. The fourth is about tangible resources. This pathway outlines the mental health implications of the provision of concrete monetary and non-monetary support, such as income protection schemes, care services, and mental health services, which are relevant in the community context (Saxena, Thornicroft, Knapp, & Whiteford, 2007).

In the context of China, the fundamental causes theory is a suitable framework in analyzing the community-level effects of urbanization on the depression of the older population. The major reason is that urbanization represents a socioeconomic and physical environment transformation for rural communities, which is closely related to community socioeconomic status. The upgrading of infrastructure and economic structure is supposed to be a direct result of land expropriation, which is followed by restructuring of a community's welfare arrangements and social networks. According to fundamental causes theory, these changes in a community's socioeconomic and physical environment can provide access to more resources that contain mental health risks on the one hand, and shape exposure to and experience of most mental health risks on the other.

3.4 Depression of older adults and urbanization in the social ecological perspective

Two competing theories on the influences of urbanization on human wellbeing have been proposed. One is the double jeopardy theory, which claims that urbanization will lead to a widening gap in human development outcomes and deteriorate the health of marginalized groups in the urban (Robert, 1999). This theory focuses on the association between socioeconomic status and the resources one can access in cities. It proposes two coexisting jeopardies to human wellbeing in the context of urbanization. The first jeopardy is based on two presumptions, namely (1) urbanization will lead to increased income inequity; and (2) the average income level in a city determines the prices of health products and services and other essential resources for human development. As such, with ongoing urbanization, income inequality increases, and in turn, more essential resources for mental wellbeing will be unaffordable for people with low incomes.

The second jeopardy is in relation to urban residents' vulnerabilities confronting the risks of a dense population and a hazardous environment resulting from urbanization. Past literature has shown that people with low socioeconomic status tend to be more vulnerable when facing urban life risks, such as environmental pollution, food security, and resources shortage (Du, Mroz, Zhai, & Popkin, 2004; Fang & Rizzo, 2012). The double jeopardy theory is supported by some empirical findings in Western countries. For instance, Bassuk et al. (2002) reported that the association between socioeconomic status and mortality in the older population was stronger in communities with higher levels of urbanization in America. However, whether it applies to the whole world is still debatable. Higher socioeconomic status inequality in urban areas is also found in China's context, while the health of the urban Chinese, including marginalized groups in urban China, is generally better than that of the rural Chinese (Zimmer & Kwong, 2004).

On the other hand, the health penalty theory proposes that the inequality in human development outcomes will be flattened by urbanization. The reasons are two-fold. First, there will be a health penalty of urbanization for the advantaged class. Although this theory recognizes the health advantages (e.g., higher income, wider access to health services) brought about by urbanization, it suggests that these health advantages can be suppressed by unhealthy lifestyles, such as high-fat food, drinking, smoking, and unsafe sex (Allender, Foster, Hutchinson, & Arambepola, 2008; Di Cesare et al., 2013). The advantaged class in the cities is more likely to be affected by these health penalties (Van de Poel, O'Donnell, & Van Doorslaer, 2012). Especially in the urbanization process of developing countries, the situation can be worsened by inadequate health services and education (Zhu, Ioannidis, Li, Jones, & Martin, 2011).

The second reason is in relation to the positive social externalities for marginalized groups in the urban areas. That is, people with low income and education may get access to health facilities and services in the urban areas due to the improvement of urban governance; moreover, they can also benefit from the social diversity of urban life, which provides them with more health guidance and information (Van de Poel et al., 2012).

To sum up, the double jeopardy theory and the health penalty theory focus on different aspects of urbanization's influences on human development outcomes. The former stresses the risks factors for the marginalized groups in the urban areas; while the latter emphasizes the positive social externalities for marginalized groups and the risks factors for the advantaged groups in the urban areas. Consensus has been reached on the fact that urbanization can bring about both health advantages and disadvantages (Gong et al., 2012). Therefore, a comprehensive theoretical framework, covering both risks and opportunities resulting from urbanization, is needed to give a full picture of the association between urbanization and mental wellbeing.

According to Bronfenbrenner (2009), the entire socio-ecological system in which one is located needs to be taken into account in order to understand human development. Five socially organized subsystems are included in the system, which is decided by the contextual nature of one's life and provides various options and sources of development. Moreover, there are bidirectional impacts within and between each subsystem. The innermost layer is the microsystem, referring to the structure with which one has direct contact. It includes individual characteristics, such as gender and age, and the institutions and groups that most directly affect one's development, such as close family members, school, and church. The second is the mesosystem, which refers to the relationships between the microsystems, such as the associations between one's parents and one's schooling experience. The third is the exosystem, which involves links between a social setting in which the individual does not have an active role and the individual's immediate context. For instance, land expropriation is usually beyond the control of rural community residents although it can affect their lives significantly. The fourth is the macrosystem, referring to the attitudes and ideologies of the culture in which one lives, such as the development stages of the country (developing or developed), socioeconomic status, poverty, and ethnicity. The final one is the chronosystem, referring to the patterning of significant events over the life course.

This research constructs the research framework with the guidance of the socio-ecological perspective. This framework disentangles China's urbanization into three dimensions of constructs, namely an individual's social identity transformation in the life course, the family living-arrangement shift, and community environment restructuring. At the individual level, through utilizing the developmental adaptation model, the effects of the mesosystem (i.e., the cluster of early-life events), the macrosystem (i.e., the *Hukou* policy), and the chronosystem (i.e., the linkage between distal and proximal life events and current depressive symptoms) are explored. At the household level, through utilizing the stress-buffering model, the effects of the microsystem (i.e., the family support and family living arrangements) are explored. At the community level, through utilizing the fundamental causes theory, the effects of the exosystem (i.e., the community physical and socioeconomic environment) are explored.

3.5 Data sources

The quantitative data used in this book is from the baseline of the China Health and Retirement Longitudinal Survey (CHARLS). This national representative survey was carried out by the joint team of the National School of Development, the Institute of Social Science Survey, and the Chinese Communist Youth League Committee of Peking University. As a key project funded by the National Natural Science Foundation, CHARLS aims to collect high-quality micro-level data that is representative of the Chinese older population and thus provides empirical evidence for analyzing population aging in China and promoting interdisciplinary research on the elderly.

The baseline national wave of CHARLS were conducted in 2011 and include about 10,000 households and 17,500 individuals in 150 counties/districts and 450 villages/resident committees. The individuals will be followed up every two years. All data will be made public one year after the end of data collection. Thus, currently four national waves of datasets (i.e., 2011 Wave 1; 2013 Wave 2; 2015 Wave 3; and 2018 Wave 4), two pilot study datasets (i.e., 2008 Pilot and 2012 Pilot), and one specific survey dataset (i.e., 2014 Life History Survey) can be found on the official website of CHALRS. It adopts multi-stage stratified PPS sampling. As an innovation of CHARLS, a software package (CHARLS-Gis) is being created to make village sampling frames.

CHARLS is based on the Health and Retirement Study (HRS) and related aging surveys such as the English Longitudinal Study of Aging (ELSA) and the Survey of Health, Aging and Retirement in Europe (SHARE). The CHARLS questionnaire includes the following modules: demographics, family structure/transfer, health status and functioning, biomarkers, health care and insurance, work, retirement and pension, income and consumption, assets (individual and household), and community-level information (Zhao et al., 2013).

A part of the qualitative data used in this book is from the author's fieldwork in Shanghai, including field visits in 51 comprehensive services centers for the elderly, two time banks, one community body and brain stimulation center, and the mutual-support care centers in a suburban district of Shanghai. Other qualitative data is from a review of the literature on the long-term care models widely adopted in Western countries and their application in China, as well as China's local models on elderly mental health promotion in the rural sector, namely the mutual-support care model, the land-for-care model, and the gatekeeper for mental health model. These cases and models will be elaborated and compared regarding their ways of dealing with local resources, cultural customs, and older people's needs. Moreover, information and analyses on how they were developed and potential limitations will be revealed.

3.6 Summary

This chapter sets out a theoretical framework and introduces data sources used in this book. The previous chapter instrumentalizes China's urbanization into three aspects, namely social identity transition in the individual life course, family living-arrangement change, and community environment restructuring. Accordingly, this chapter reviews theories that associate the three levels of factors and depression of older adults, respectively. After comparison of the competing theories, the developmental adaptation mode, stress-buffering model, and the fundamental causes theory are selected as the guiding theories to explore each of the focal associations. Moreover, through a review of the theories that either depict the positive or negative influences of urbanization on mental health, this chapter shows the necessity of using a comprehensive framework to disentangle urbanization's influences on Chinese rural older people at the individual, household, and community levels. Following the introduction and adaptation of the social ecological perspective, this chapter introduces the data sources of this book, including the China Health and Retirement Longitudinal Survey, the author's fieldwork in Shanghai, the literature on the long-term care models widely adopted in Western countries and their application in China, as well as China's local models on elderly mental health promotion in the rural sector.

References

Acevedo, G. A., Ellison, C. G., & Xu, X. (2014). Is it really religion? Comparing the main and stress-buffering effects of religious and secular civic engagement on psychological distress. *Society and Mental Health, 4*(2), 111–128. 2156869313520558. doi:10.1177/2156869313520558

Allender, S., Foster, C., Hutchinson, L., & Arambepola, C. (2008). Quantification of urbanization in relation to chronic diseases in developing countries: A systematic review. *Journal of Urban Health, 85*(6), 938–951.

Armitage, C. J., & Conner, M. (2000). Social cognition models and health behaviour: A structured review. *Psychology and Health, 15*(2), 173–189. doi:10.1080/08870440008400299

Bandura, A. (2012). On the functional properties of perceived self-efficacy revisited. *Journal of Management, 38*(1), 9–44. doi:10.1177/0149206311410606

Bandura, A. (2001). Social cognitive theory: An agentic perspective. *Annual Review of Psychology, 52*(1), 1–26. doi:10.1146/annurev.psych.52.1.1

Bartholomew, K., & Horowitz, L. M. (1991). Attachment styles among young adults: A test of a four-category model. *Journal of Personality and Social Psychology, 61*(2), 226. doi:10.1037/0022-3514.61.2.226

Bassuk, S. S., Berkman, L. F., & Amick, B. C. (2002). Socioeconomic status and mortality among the elderly: Findings from four US communities. *American Journal of Epidemiology, 155*(6), 520–533. doi:10.1093/aje/155.6.520

Biao, X. (2007). How far are the left-behind left behind? A preliminary study in rural China. *Population, Space and Place, 13*(3), 179–191. doi:10.1002/psp.437

Bronfenbrenner, U. (2009). *The Ecology of Human Development: Experiments by Nature and Design*: Cambridge, MA: Harvard University Press.

Cohen, S. (2004). Social relationships and health. *American Psychologist, 59*(8), 676. doi:10.1037/0003-066X.59.8.676

Dannefer, D. (2003). Whose life course is it, anyway? Diversity and "linked lives" in global perspective. In *Invitation to the Life Course: Toward New Understandings of Later Life* (pp. 259–268). New York: Routledge.

Di Cesare, M., Khang, Y.-H., Asaria, P., Blakely, T., Cowan, M. J., Farzadfar, F., … Msyamboza, K. P. (2013). Inequalities in non-communicable diseases and effective responses. *The Lancet, 381*(9866), 585–597. doi:10.1016/S0140-6736(12)61851-0

DiPrete, T. A., & Eirich, G. M. (2006). Cumulative advantage as a mechanism for inequality: A review of theoretical and empirical developments. *Annual Review of Sociology, 32*, 271–297. doi:10.1146/annurev.soc.32.061604.123127

Du, S., Mroz, T. A., Zhai, F., & Popkin, B. M. (2004). Rapid income growth adversely affects diet quality in China: Particularly for the poor! *Social Science & Medicine, 59*(7), 1505–1515. doi:10.1016/j.socscimed.2004.01.021

Elder, G. H. (1998). The life course as developmental theory. *Child Development*, *69*(1), 1–12. doi:10.1111/j.1467-8624.1998.tb06128.x

Fang, H., & Rizzo, J. A. (2012). Does inequality in China affect health differently in high-versus low-income households? *Applied Economics*, *44*(9), 1081–1090.

Frishman, N. (2012). The contribution of three social psychological theories: Fundamental cause theory, stress process model, and social cognitive theory to the understanding of health disparities: A longitudinal comparison. Graduate Theses and Dissertations. Iowa State University. 12807.

Fry, P. S., & Debats, D. L. (2006). Sources of life strengths as predictors of late-life mortality and survivorship. *The International Journal of Aging and Human Development*, *62*(4), 303–334.

Gong, P., Liang, S., Carlton, E. J., Jiang, Q., Wu, J., Wang, L., & Remais, J. V. (2012). Urbanisation and health in China. *The Lancet*, *379*(9818), 843–852. doi:10.1016/S0140-6736(11)61878-3

Kawachi, I., & Berkman, L. (2001). Social ties and mental health. *Journal of Urban Health*, *78*(3), 458–467. doi:10.1093/jurban/78.3.458

Marshall, V. W. (2009). Theory informing public policy: The life course perspective as a policy tool. In V. L. Bengtson, D. Gans, N. Putney, & M. Silverstein (Eds.), *Handbook of Theories of Aging* (pp. 573–593). New York: Springer.

Martin, P., & Martin, M. (2002). Proximal and distal influences on development: The model of developmental adaptation. *Developmental Review*, *22*(1), 78–96.

National Bureau of Statistics of China. (2015). *Survey Report on China's Migrant Workers*. Retrieved from Beijing, China: National Bureau of Statistics of China.

Pearlin, L. I., Menaghan, E. G., Lieberman, M. A., & Mullan, J. T. (1981). The stress process. *Journal of Health and Social Behavior*, *22*(4), 337–356.

Phelan, J. C., Link, B. G., Diez-Roux, A., Kawachi, I., & Levin, B. (2004). "Fundamental causes" of social inequalities in mortality: A test of the theory. *Journal of Health and Social Behavior*, *45*(3), 265–285. doi:10.1177/002214650404500303

Phelan, J. C., Link, B. G., & Tehranifar, P. (2010). Social conditions as fundamental causes of health inequalities theory, evidence, and policy implications. *Journal of Health and Social Behavior*, *51*(1 suppl), S28–S40. doi:10.1177/0022146510383498

Poon, C. Y. M. (2013). Meeting the mental health needs of older adults using the attachment perspective. In A. N. Danquah & K. Berry (Eds.), *Attachment Theory in Adult Mental Health: A Guide to Clinical Practice* (pp. 183–196). New York: Routledge.

Poon, L. W., Clayton, G. M., Martin, P., Johnson, M. A., Courtenay, B. C., Sweaney, A. L., … Thielman, S. B. (1992). The Georgia centenarian study. *The International Journal of Aging and Human Development*, *34*(1), 1–17.

Raffaelli, M., Andrade, F. C., Wiley, A. R., Sanchez-Armass, O., Edwards, L. L., & Aradillas-Garcia, C. (2013). Stress, social support, and depression: A test of the stress-buffering hypothesis in a mexican sample. *Journal of Research on Adolescence*, *23*(2), 283–289. doi:10.1111/jora.12006

Robert, S. A. (1999). Socioeconomic position and health: The independent contribution of community socioeconomic context. *Annual Review of Sociology*, *25*, 489–516.

Saxena, S., Thornicroft, G., Knapp, M., & Whiteford, H. (2007). Resources for mental health: Scarcity, inequity, and inefficiency. *The Lancet, 370*(9590), 878–889. doi:10.1016/S0140-6736(07)61239-2

Shields, M. A., Price, S. W., & Wooden, M. (2009). Life satisfaction and the economic and social characteristics of neighbourhoods. *Journal of Population Economics, 22*(2), 421–443. doi:10.1007/s00148-007-0146-7

Turner, R. J. (2010). Understanding health disparities: The promise of the stress process model. In W. Avison, C. S. Aneshensel, S. Schieman, & B. Wheaton (Eds.), *Advances in the Conceptualization of the Stress Process* (pp. 3–21). New York: Springer.

Van de Poel, E., O'Donnell, O., & Van Doorslaer, E. (2012). Is there a health penalty of China's rapid urbanization? *Health Economics, 21*(4), 367–385. doi:10.1002/hec.1717

Zeng, Z., & Xie, Y. (2014). The effects of grandparents on children's schooling: Evidence from rural China. *Demography, 51*(2), 599–617. doi:10.1007/s13524-013-0275-4

Zhao, Y., Strauss, J., Yang, G., Giles, J., Hu, P. P., Hu, Y., ... Wang, Y. (2013). China health and retirement longitudinal study: 2011–2012 national baseline users' guide Retrieved from http://charls.ccer.edu.cn/uploads/document/2011-charls-wave1/application/CHARLS_users__guide_ofnationalbaseline_survey-js-yz-Lei_wang-js_ys_js-ys-zhao_ys_20130407.pdf

Zhu, Y.-G., Ioannidis, J. P., Li, H., Jones, K. C., & Martin, F. L. (2011). Understanding and harnessing the health effects of rapid urbanization in China. *Environmental Science & Technology, 45*(12), 5099–5104. doi:10.1021/es2004254

Zimmer, Z., & Kwong, J. (2004). Socioeconomic status and health among older adults in rural and urban China. *Journal of Aging and Health, 16*(1), 44–70. doi:10.1177/0898264303260440

4 Urbanization and depression of Chinese rural older population in the social ecological perspective

4.1 Life transitions and depression of the Chinese rural older population

This chapter examines how distal life events (i.e., childhood adversities) and proximal life events (i.e., social identity transformation in urbanization) are associated with current human development outcomes (i.e., depression) for the Chinese rural mature and older population. It aims to reveal how the proxy of urbanization at the individual level, namely social identity transformation in the life course, has moderated the association between childhood life adversities and depression in later life.

According to the developmental adaptation model (DAM) proposed by Martin and Martin (2002), human development and aging are lifelong processes, in which personal resources and experiential factors optimize adaptation. That is, distal life events may influence the human development outcome in later life, and this association can be affected by the intervening variables such as individual, social, and economic resources and proximal life events. Based on these propositions, this study sets out the following three research hypotheses:

(a) As a distal life stressor, adverse childhood experiences are significantly associated with depressive symptoms in later life;
(b) As a proximal significant life event and resource, social identity transformation in the urbanization process is significantly associated with depressive symptoms in later life;
(c) Social identity transformation is a significant moderator of the association between childhood adversity and depressive symptoms in later life.

This analysis based itself on a subsample of the China Health and Retirement Longitudinal Study (CHARLS) – Baseline. The sample selection criteria

DOI: 10.4324/9781003248767-4

were three-fold, including (1) with the first *Hukou* being rural; (2) being 45 or above; and (3) spent the childhood period (i.e., before 16) in the rural sector. The information of 14,681 respondents was retrieved after applying the three criteria. These mature and older adults were in similar positions on the social ladder in their early lives, namely they were born and raised in rural China where socioeconomic status and lifestyle were quite uniform under the communist totalitarianism before the late 1970s. Therefore, it would be interesting to investigate how the profound urbanization that occurred in the following three decades changed their life courses and, in turn, has differentiated their mental wellbeing.

Modern China's urbanization started in the late 1970s, along with the implementation of the Reform and Opening Up policies, and has accelerated since the late 1990s. This timing coincides with the working age of the current Chinese mature and older population. Urbanization could bring them a lifestyle, a career, and living arrangements substantially different from those in the countryside, and thus could affect their mental wellbeing significantly. Therefore, this group of the Chinese population is very relevant for research on the moderating effects of urbanization on the association between CAs and depressive symptoms in later life.

4.1.1 Measures

4.1.1.1 Childhood adversity

Seven variables were included as the indicators for CAs in the study, according to the existing literature on CA and in consideration of China's contextual features. They were coded into dummy variables, with "1" representing "without the CA" and "0" representing "with the CA". The first and the second indicator are "father death" and "mother death", respectively, meaning that the respondent experienced the death of a parent before 16 years old. The third indicator is "famine", which was coded according to Li's (1994) summarization of the ten most serious famines that happened in China between 1840 and 1949, as well as the Great Chinese Famine of 1959–1961. Respondents born in a famine year or the next year after a famine year (i.e., spent the uterus period in a famine year) were coded with this childhood adversity. This coding method is guided by the "fetal origin hypothesis" (Barker, 1997). The fourth is "no schooling", which references that the respondent had no schooling experience before the age of 16. The fifth indicator is "parental illiteracy", which describes that the respondent was raised by illiterate parents. The sixth is "disability", referring to the fact that a respondent had a physical disability, brain injury, hearing or vision problem, or speech disorder during childhood. The final one is "poor health", referring to the fact that a respondent's childhood health condition was poor, which is retrospective information reported by the respondents themselves. The seven indicators for CA fall into three categories: "father death", "mother death", and "famine" belong to life trauma; "no schooling" and "parental illiteracy" are about socioeconomic status; while "disability" and "poor health" are about physical and functional health.

4.1.1.2 Social identity

Existing literature has proposed a number of methods to categorize and measure urbanization. These methods are usually about the modernization of economic and family life, location of residence, and features of the neighborhood environment (Brown, Cromartie, & Kulcsar, 2004; Ou, Li, Liu, & Chen, 2004). Since China's urbanization is largely driven by institutional forces, this analysis utilized a measure that combines information on respondents' neighborhood type and *Hukou* status. Three types of social identity were identified accordingly: (1) the non-urbanized, meaning that the respondents stayed in the rural sector and held the rural *Hukou* all the time; (2) the semi-urbanized, meaning that the respondents were living in an urban neighborhood while still holding a rural *Hukou*; and (3) the fully urbanized, referring that the respondents had obtained the urban *Hukou*. This categorization is not new: due to the persistence of the *Hukou* system, a lot of attention has been paid to migrants who live in the urban areas while being denied access to equal civil rights as local urban residents. This phenomenon has compelled many scholars to describe China's urbanization as "semi-urbanization" or "pseudo-urbanization" (Wang, 2006).

4.1.1.3 Depression

The 10-item Center for Epidemiological Studies Depression Short Form (CES-D-10) was applied to measure depressive symptoms of the mature and older population in this study. As a widely used scale, the 10-item version of CES-D has demonstrated strong psychometric properties, including predictive accuracy and high correlations with the original 20-item version, in community populations (Björgvinsson, Kertz, Bigda-Peyton, McCoy, & Aderka, 2013). Table 4.1 shows the content of the original 20-item version and the revised 10-item version.

The scale requires the participants to rate their feelings and behaviors according to the situations that have happened in the previous week. The responses are four-fold, including "rarely or none of the time" (less than 1 day), "some or a little of the time" (1–2 days), "occasionally or a moderate amount of time" (3–4 days), and "most or all of the time" (5–7 days).

Table 4.1 CES-D 20 and CES-D 10

CES-D – 20	CES-D – 10
I was bothered by things that usually don't bother me.	I was bothered by things that usually don't bother me.
I did not feel like eating; my appetite was poor.	
I felt that I could not shake off the blues even with help from my family or friends.	I had trouble keeping my mind on what I was doing.
I felt I was just as good as other people.*	
I had trouble keeping my mind on what I was doing.	I felt depressed.
I felt depressed.	
I felt that everything I did was an effort.	I felt that everything I did was an effort.
I felt hopeful about the future.*	
I thought my life had been a failure.	I felt hopeful about the future.*
I felt fearful.	
My sleep was restless.	I felt fearful.
I was happy.*	
I talked less than usual.	My sleep was restless.
I felt lonely.	
People were unfriendly.	I was happy.*
I enjoyed life.*	
I had crying spells.	I felt lonely.
I felt sad.	
I felt that people dislike me.	I could not get "going".
I could not get "going".	

Each of the responses is coded a score, namely 0, 1, and 2, respectively. It is worth noting that the items with an asterisk in Table 4.1 would be coded reversely. That is, the range of the total score for the CES-D 10 is between 0 and 30, with a higher score representing higher depression. Based on the responses from the CHARLS – Baseline, the Cronbach α coefficient for the scale is 0.796, which indicates a desirable reliability in the current sample.

4.1.2 Analyses

The statistical analysis of this research comprises two steps. Latent class analysis (LCA) was first used to identify the number and nature of the sub-types of the respondents' CAs. LCA compared the fit indices of four models, namely a two-class latent class model through to a five-class model. Four fit indices were examined to select the optimal number of latent classes, including Akaike information criterion (AIC), Bayesian information criterion (BIC), Lo-Mendell-Rubin's adjusted LR test (LRT), and entropy measures (Nylund, Asparouhov, & Muthén, 2007). The lower the values of AIC and BIC, the better the fit a model has. As for Lo-Mendell-Rubin's LRT, a non-significant observed value ($p > .05$) indicates that the model with one fewer class should be accepted. Finally, entropy is a standardized measure of how accurately participants are classified. Entropy values can range from 0 to 1 with higher values indicating a better classification.

The second step of statistical analysis involves a factorial analysis of a covariance model. It included the urbanization status and the CA class membership for the respondents. Gender and age were put into the model as covariates, in order to reduce within-group error variance and to eliminate confounds (Field, 2009). Now that the existing literature has consistently reported that males and females can be influenced by childhood adversities to different degrees (Wainwright & Surtees, 2002), scarce evidence has been found in the Chinese context. Moreover, the wide age range of the respondents (i.e., aged 45 or above) necessitates the consideration of age. The factorial analysis of covariance in this study served two goals. One is to examine whether various CA latent classes have significant differences in depressive symptoms. The other is to investigate whether social identity can have a significant moderation effect on the association between depressive symptoms and the CA class membership.

4.1.3 Results

The descriptive statistics of the research samples are presented in Table 4.2. As with the demographics, 51.2% of respondents were female, the average age was 59.1 years old, and 87.0% of them were married with a spouse alive. Regarding social identity, 66.1% of them were non-urbanized; 22.9% were semi-urbanized; and only 11.0% were fully urbanized. The respondents had quite a differentiated endorsement rate with regard to the seven CAs: with "parental illiteracy" experienced by as many as 58.5% of respondents and "disability" experienced by only 2.1% of them.

4.1.3.1 Latent classes of childhood adversity

The first step of the analysis, namely the latent class analysis, reported the clustered nature of the CAs. Table 4.3 presents the five fit indices of the four latent class analyses. The three-class model was found to have the optimal model fit: the AIC and BIC were lower than the two-class model, the p value for LRT indicated that the four-class model is not significantly better than the three-class (and so the three-class solution should be preferred on the basis of parsimony), and the entropy value is acceptable.

Table 4.4 presents the distribution of the seven CAs among the three latent classes. Class 1 was the largest group, with 9,337 members and accounting for 63.6% of the total research samples. Compared with the other two latent classes, Class 1 featured moderate to low probability of

Table 4.2 Descriptive statistics of the respondents for the first sub-study

Variable	Observations (%)	Mean	SD*
Sample size	14,681	–	–
Age (45–101)	14,681	59.1	9.9
Gender			
Female	7,522 (51.2)	–	–
Male	7,147 (48.7)	–	–
Marital status			
Married	12,766 (87.0)	–	–
Separated/divorced	150 (1.0)	–	–
Widowed	1,617 (11.0)	–	–
Never married	147 (1.0)	–	–
Depression score (0–30)	12,649	8.8	6.4
Urbanization status	14,617	–	–
Non-urbanized	9,658 (66.1)	–	–
Semi-urbanized	3,350 (22.9)	–	–
Fully urbanized	1,609 (11.0)	–	–
CAs			
Father death	1,984 (13.5)	–	–
Mother death	3,412 (23.2)	–	–
Famine	2,483 (16.9)	–	–
No schooling	4,450 (30.3)	–	–
Parental illiteracy	8,591 (58.5)		
Poor health	1,055 (7.2)	–	–
Disability	313 (2.1)	–	–

Notes: SD = standard deviation.

Table 4.3 Fit indices for the latent class analysis of childhood adversities

Model	AIC	BIC	*p for LRT*	Entropy
2 classes	84,962	85,076	<.001	.694
3 classes	84,195	84,370	<.001	.721
4 classes	84,165	84,400	.053	.767
5 classes	84,154	84,450	.386	.571

Table 4.4 Distribution of the childhood adversities in the three latent classes

	Class 1 (% within class)	Class 2 (% within class)	Class 3 (% within class)
Father death	564 (6.04)	193 (4.71)	1,226 (100.00)
Mother death	1,539 (16.48)	656 (16.01)	1,214 (99.02)
Famine	1,633 (17.49)	619 (15.11)	228 (18.60)
Parental illiteracy	4,795 (51.35)	3,086 (75.32)	710 (57.91)
No schooling	2 (.02)	4,094 (99.93)	354 (28.87)
Disability	168 (1.80)	122 (2.98)	22 (1.79)
Poor health	632 (6.77)	346 (8.45)	77 (6.28)

Notes: N = 9,337 for Class 1. N = 4,097 for Class 2. N = 1,226 for Class 3.

having the seven CAs. Class 2 and Class 3 accounted for 27.9% and 8.4% of the total research samples, respectively. On the one hand, Class 2 was found to have the highest probability of having "parental illiteracy", "no schooling", "disability", and "poor health", which are indicators of childhood socioeconomic and health status. On the other hand, Class 3 was most likely to have "father death", "mother death", and "famine", which are life disasters. According to the findings, this study labeled Class 1, Class 2, and Class 3 as "normal childhood class", "low childhood SES and health class", and "traumatic childhood class", respectively.

4.1.3.2 Depression variances of the three CA classes

The LCA generated CA class membership for research samples, which became an independent variable in the following factorial analysis of covariance. The CA class membership was found to have significant association with the depressive symptoms of research samples, F $(2, 12,561) = 4.20$, $p = .015$; Bonferroni comparisons of the three classes indicated that the estimated marginal means for the depression score of the "low childhood SES and health class" ($M = 8.95$, 95% CI [8.58, 9.32]) was significantly higher than that of the "traumatic childhood class" ($M = 8.09$, 95% CI [7.60, 8.57]) ($p = .016$), while it is not significantly higher than that of the "normal childhood class" ($M = 8.49$, 95% CI [8.32, 8.65]) ($p = .076$) at .05 level; moreover, no significant difference in the estimated marginal means for the depression score was reported between the "low childhood SES and health class" and the "normal childhood class" ($p = .365$).

4.1.3.3 Effects of covariates and urbanization status

Assuming urbanization as significantly moderating the association between depressive symptoms and the CAs, this study included social identity and CA latent class membership into the factorial analysis of covariance as fixed factors, with covariating age and gender (see Table 4.5). Regarding the covariates, both age (B = .08; F = 171.48; $p < .001$) and gender (B = 2.11; F = 353.29; $p < .001$) had significant correlation with the depressive symptoms of the research samples; moreover, the B coefficients showed that the depression score was higher for females than for males and tended to increase with age. The results also showed that social identity was significantly associated with depressive symptoms (F = 3.00; $p = .05$); the higher the urbanized social identity, the lower the depression score; and the interaction between social identity and the CAs had a significant effect on the depressive symptoms (F = 4.27; $p = .002$), which revealed that the social identity significantly moderated the association between CAs and depressive symptoms.

Table 4.5 Tests of between-subjects effects

	Type III sum of squares	df	Mean square	F	Sig.
Corrected model	23,791	10	2,379	60.24	< .001
Intercept	82.77	1	82.77	2.10	.148
Age	6,772	1	6,772	171.48	<.001
Gender	13,953	1	13,953	353.29	< .001
CA class membership	332	2	166	4.20	.015
Social identity	237	2	119	3.00	.050
Social identity* CA membership	675	4	169	4.27	.002
Error	496,043	12,560	39.49		

Notes: N = 12,571. df = degree of freedom. Sig. = significance. Unstandardized coefficient (B) for age is .08, for gender is 2.11. R squared = .046.

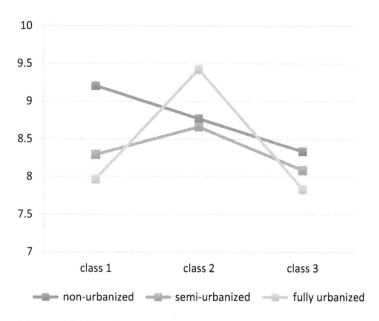

Figure 4.1 Estimated marginal means for the depressive symptoms score.

Figure 4.1 presents the results of estimated marginal means for the depression score. Among the non-urbanized, Class 3, namely the traumatic childhood class, reported the lowest depression score, Class 2 (i.e., the low childhood SES and health class) reported the second lowest, and Class 1 (i.e., the normal childhood class) had the highest depression score. However, this trajectory did not apply to the fully urbanized and the semi-urbanized, in which Class 2 had the highest depression score while Class 1 ranked second. It is also worth noting that though the fully urbanized and the semi-urbanized had a similar trajectory, they had quite a different fluctuation.

4.1.4 Discussion

In line with past literature, current research has reported the significant association between CAs and depressive symptoms. The latent class analysis generated a more detailed picture for the association. First, this analysis demonstrated the clustered nature of CAs. It is reported that "early father death" and "early mother death" clustered with "born in a famine year"; and "no schooling experience" with "both parents illiterate" clustered with "disability" and "poor physical health in childhood". This latent structure led to the labeling of the three classes. Past literature supports the CA clustering found in this research. Empirical studies on Chinese famines have consistently reported a higher mortality rate of middle-aged adults than other age groups, and Chen and Zhou (2007) interpreted this phenomenon as the result of Chinese traditional family values that require the adults to give away limited food to the older generation and their children in hard times. This may explain the cluster of early death of parents born in a famine year. Moreover, a large volume of literature has documented the association between socioeconomic status and physical and functional status (Bradley & Corwyn, 2002), which can explain their cluster in this study.

This study also reported the variances in depressive symptoms between different CA latent classes. It is worth noting that the traumatic childhood class had the lowest estimated marginal mean of the depression score, controlling for age and gender. The reasons are three-fold. The first is in relation to support from extended family, which may function as a safety net and buffer the negative effects of parent loss. According to Zeng (1986), joint family was a prevalent family form in rural China before the 1980s, and in this type of family, married siblings either lived under the same roof or lived close by (e.g., door-to-door) when they formed separate family units. This context facilitated the mutual help of close family members. Further, the Chinese extended kinship system was likely to be strengthened in dire living circumstances (Chen, 1985). In other words, other family members might take on the role of parents when children are orphaned and resources from various family members might be pooled together for joint economic survival in times of famine.

The second reason is given by the selection effect hypothesis. Gørgens et al. (2012) found that people surviving traumatic events, including famine, were actually healthier and stronger in later life and thus can cope with stressors better. Other indicators in the CHARLS datasets also supported the health advantage of people who survived traumatic childhoods. For example, they reported the highest rate of ranking current health as good and very good and the lowest rate of poor health in childhood.

The third is about education. A much higher proportion of respondents belonging to Class 3 had schooling experience than those in Class 2. It is well recognized that education is an effective preventive factor for depression (Werner & Smith, 2001). According to Fergusson and Horwood (2003), higher education is associated with better problem-solving skills, social networks, intelligence, and occupation, which may offset or reverse the negative psychological effects of childhood adversities in adult life.

Significant moderating effects of social identity on the association between the CAs and current depressive symptoms were reported for the Chinese mature and older population. Past literature also demonstrated the significant role of the macro social environment in influencing individuals' mental wellbeing, such as the research on the baby boomer cohort and the children born in the Great Depression period (Elder, 1999; Wilson, 2006). Though urbanization generally decreased the level of depressive symptoms for the mature and older adults, its moderating effects on the correlation between CAs and depressive symptoms deserve a more detailed analysis and policy attention.

Different trajectories of depressive symptoms were reported for the research samples of the three CAs classes according to their different social identities. Regarding the fully urbanized and the semi-urbanized, Class 2 (low childhood SES and health class) reported the highest depressive symptoms score, which was especially so for the fully urbanized. The institutional inequalities for rural migrants in urban China may explain the result. For a Chinese rural *Hukou* holder, transforming into an urban social identity means participating in an unjust competition that requires overcoming various institutional obstacles. A number of family and individual backgrounds, such as education, family background, health and functional status, may all play a significant role. Therefore, as a result of the various institutional exclusion mechanisms shaped by the *Hukou* system and the deeply rooted social stigma on the rural identity, the fully urbanized and the semi-urbanized who had a low education and family background could face more obstacles in the process of upward social mobility. At the same time, China's urbanization is instrumental rationality based, with an emphasis on economic productivity and efficiency. As with the resulting social issues, such as social protection mechanism construction and inclusion of the underprivileged, however, China still has a long way to go (Leung, 2006).

On the other hand, the class reporting the highest depressive symptoms score among the non-urbanized was the normal childhood class. This may be explained by status inconsistencies. These people might be in a better socioeconomic status than the other two groups in the childhood period; however, their current social identity was lower than that of the other two groups. In Chinese society, an urban social identity has both socioeconomic and cultural implications. That is to say, it does not only mean wider access to economic opportunities and resources, but also implies superior psychological advantages, mainly a result of assumed higher education and cultural taste (Wang, 2001). To avoid this stigma, it is necessary to break the institutional obstacles setting for maintaining the rural–urban segregation in China and further to allow for equal development opportunities to the rural sector. On the other hand, it is necessary to encourage the social identity transformation of rural people considering the still large potential for urbanization in China.

Gender difference in depressive symptoms has been consistently reported by the existing literature. That is, females are more likely to suffer from depression than males (Luppa et al., 2012). This study also echoed the past literature by reporting the female preponderance in depressive symptoms. The reasons can be two-fold. First, some artefactual factors, including thresholds for caseness, measurement procedures, course of illness, and symptom reporting, may lead to the result (Piccinelli & Wilkinson, 2000). According to Sonnenberg et al. (2000), females and males have different ways of self-expression. That is, females are more likely to speak out about negative feelings while males are more likely to deny and instead act them out through suicide or alcoholism. The second reason is in relation to genuine social and psychological determinants, such as sociocultural roles and supports, coping skills, and vulnerability to life events. Luppa et al. (2012) also reported the non-significant role of genetic or biological factors on the emergence of gender variance in depression.

This research also reported the significant association between age and depressive symptoms. According to (Blazer, 2003), this can be attributed to lower socioeconomic status, higher prevalence and incidence of health and functional problems, and a higher proportion of females in the aging population. However, this finding is not indisputable. For instance, Djernes (2006) did not find a significant association between depression and older age in his review of the literature on depression in later life. Further, though many studies found that depressive symptoms were more prevalent among the oldest old, they reported that no more frequency or less frequency was found in general late life than in midlife (Charles, Reynolds, & Gatz, 2001). These contentions necessitate further investigations on whether there is a real increase of depressive symptoms in the older population.

This research enriches the understandings on the association between adverse childhood experience and mental wellbeing in later life. It is proposed that the debates over the association are largely due to ignorance of the fact that social identity transformation happens in-between the life stages. Based on the developmental adaptation model, this study investigated the aging of people as a process incorporating distal and proximal life stressors, with the aim of linking childhood life with middle- and older-age life through the social identity transformation happening in between. This method streamlines the association between adverse childhood experience and human development outcomes in later life.

Findings of this research can also shed light on significant implications for other countries undergoing urbanization processes. Along with the deepening of urbanization and population aging around the globe, especially in the low- and middle-income countries, increasing attention has been paid to the intertwining of these two major demographic transformations (Beard & Petitot, 2010). This has evolved into a public concern as how to shape a process of urbanization that facilitates better human development outcomes in later life. Our study shows that although urbanization generally contributes to better psychological wellbeing, it can worsen the psychological wellbeing of people with certain life backgrounds. In particular, it was revealed that the higher the extent of urbanization, the higher the level of psychological disadvantages for people with a low childhood SES and poor health compared with their peers. To avoid cumulative disadvantage, socially inclusive policies should be introduced within the urbanization context, with special attention being paid to those who are disadvantaged in terms of family and individual socioeconomic status, health, or physical function.

4.2 Family living arrangements and depression of the Chinese rural older population

This analysis is to examine how the proxy of urbanization at the household level, namely the living-arrangement shift, is associated with family support and the depressive symptoms of the Chinese rural mature and older population. Specifically, it examines whether the household living-arrangement shift resulting from the out-migration of the children's generation has negative associations with the depressive symptoms of the Chinese rural mature and older adults; and whether the negative associations are compensated for by family-level resources.

According to the stress-buffering model, family characteristics and family-level risks are associated with individuals' mental health; moreover, the association can be mediated by family and personal resources. Based on the propositions, two study hypotheses are raised as below:

(a) For Chinese rural middle-aged and older people, living alongside children is associated with lower levels of depression;

(b) Family resources, namely family socioeconomic status, material support, and emotional support, can compensate for the negative effects of out-migration of children on the depression of the rural middle-aged and older people.

This study based itself on a subsample of the China Health and Retirement Longitudinal Study (CHARLS). Three inclusion criteria were applied for the selection of the needed subsample. They are: (1) aged at 45 or above; (2) living in the countryside; and (3) with one or more adult children. Also, since this analysis examined the material support transferred from children and other family members, research subjects only having children migrating for educational purposes were excluded. A total of 9,225 samples were left after applying these inclusion and exclusion criteria.

4.2.1 Measures

4.2.1.1 Independent variables

This study includes three family-level buffering resources, namely household socioeconomic status, material support, and emotional support from family members. The household socioeconomic status is measured by household yearly income, which is categorized into 11, namely "none", "under 2,000 RMB (1 USD roughly equals 6.2 RMB)", "between 2,000 and 5,000 RMB", "between 5,000 and 10,000 RMB", "between 10,000 and 20,000 RMB", "between 20,000 and 50,000 RMB", "between 50,000 and 100,000 RMB", "between 100,000 and 150,000 RMB", "between 150,000 and 200,000 RMB", "between 200,000 and 300,000 RMB", and "above 300,000 RMB". The family material support includes regular and irregular monetary and in-kind transfers from children, parents and parents-in-law, and other relatives. The in-kind support is transformed into a cash value reported by the recipients. Since the distribution of the total value of monetary and in-kind transfers is highly skewed, the logarithm of the RMB amount (+1) is applied to represent this variable. The variable "frequency of contacts with non-coresident children" was made the proxy for the emotional support. The frequency was categorized into nine hierarchical groups, namely ranging from "almost every day" (coded as 9) to "almost never" (coded as 1). The frequency of contact of coresident children was coded as 9. An average score was taken provided the respondent had multiple children.

Another independent variable is household living-arrangement type. Based on the presence or absence of the children's generation, all the research subjects are first categorized into three groups, namely "empty nest", "skipped-generation family", and "living with children". In the empty-nest family, no child or grandchild generation is present while the research subjects may live alone, with a spouse, or with other relatives such as a parent. In the "skipped-generation family", no member of the children's generation is present while the research subjects were living with grandchildren. The "living with children" category includes all living arrangements featuring the presence of one or more members in the children's generation. Then, based on the interaction of this categorization and the status of child migration (i.e., with or without a child migrating to other counties/cities), five household living arrangements are reached, including (1) empty-nest family without child migration (L1); (2) empty-nest family with child migration (L2); (3) skipped-generation family (L3); (4) living alongside all children (L4); and (5) living with some children aside while others have migrated (L5).

4.2.1.2 Dependent variable

The 10-item Center for Epidemiological Studies Depression Short Form (CES-D-10) is used to measure depressive symptoms in this study. As a widely used measure, the 10-item version of CES-D has demonstrated strong psychometric properties, including predictive accuracy and high correlations with the original 20-item version, in community populations (Björgvinsson et al., 2013).

4.2.1.3 Control variables

The control variables include age (in years), gender, educational level (1 = illiterate, 2 = elementary school or equivalent, 3 = middle school or above), self-rated health (5 = excellent, 4 = very good, 3 = good, 2 = fair, 1 = poor), status of instrumental activities of daily living (IADL) (number of IADL disability), and self-rated income level (1= very high, 2 = relatively high, 3 = average, 4 = relatively poor, 5 = poor).

4.2.2 Statistical analyses

The analysis process of this study was divided into two steps. First, an analysis of variance (ANOVA) was conducted to examine whether there was significant difference among people with the five household living arrangements on depressive symptoms, household income level, and family material support. Second, a multiple regression was conducted, which aims to examine whether family resources and household living arrangements are significantly associated with depressive symptoms, after controlling for the socio-demographic variables.

4.2.3 Results

Table 4.6 presents the descriptive statistics of the respondents. Regarding the demographics statistics, it is reported that 51.2% of respondents were female, the average age was 59.5 years old, and about one-third (35.0%) of them were illiterate. Turning to the living-arrangement type distribution, the share of "empty-nest family without child migration" (L1), "empty-nest family with child migration" (L2), "skipped-generation family" (L3), "living with all children aside" (L4), and "living with some children aside while others migrated" (L5) is 15.2%, 20.1%, 7.7%, 41.6%, and 15.4%, respectively.

Table 4.7 presents the results of a series of ANOVAs, which showed whether there were significant differences in depression, demographic characteristics, and family resources among the five types of living arrangements. There were significant differences among the five types of living arrangements on depression ($F = 9.57$, $p < .001$), household income ($F = 42.15$, $p < .001$), and material support ($F = 2.52$, $p < .04$). Specifically, respondents with L4, namely those who were living with all their children, had significantly lower depression ($p < .001$) than respondents with all other

Table 4.6 Descriptive statistics of the respondents for the second sub-study

Variable	Observations (%)	Mean	Standard deviation
Sample size	9,255	–	–
Gender			
Male	4,505 (48.7)	–	–
Female	4,743 (51.2)	–	–
Age (45–100)	9,255	59.5	9.6
Education			
Illiterate	3,237 (35.0)	–	–
Elementary	3,873 (41.9)	–	–
Middle school or above	2,139 (23.1)	–	–
SRH* (1–5)	9,196	3.19	.96
IADL* (1 = with disability)	1,962 (21.2)	–	–
SRI* (1–5)	8,497	3.55	.77
Household income (1–11)	9,255	4.98	2.59
Material support	9,224	12.27	.13
Emotional support	9,106	5.88	2.54
Living-arrangement type			
L1	1,407 (15.2)	–	–
L2	1,864 (20.1)	–	–
L3	709 (7.7)	–	–
L4	3,854 (41.6)	–	–
L5	1,421 (15.4)	–	–
Depression score (0–30)	8,008	9.32	6.55

Notes: SRH = self-rated health; IADL = instrumental activities of daily living; SRI = self-rated income level.

Table 4.7 Means of depressive symptoms score, demographics, and family resources by living arrangement types ($N = 9,255$)

	L1	L2	L3	L4	L5
	$N = 1,407$	$N = 1,864$	$N = 709$	$N = 3,854$	$N = 1,421$
	M / %	M / %	M / %	M / %	M / %
Depression	9.22	9.72	10.09	8.84	9.76
Household income	5.14	5.50	5.28	4.62	4.97
Material support	12.27	12.27	12.28	12.27	12.26
Emotional support	4.53	5.20	5.64	6.87	5.47
Female	51.7%	50.0%	52.2%	51.2%	52.0%
Age	63.79	61.63	60.72	56.96	58.68
Illiterate	39.9%	35.3%	37.8%	33.5%	32.7%
Poor health	34.0%	37.1%	37.2%	34.9%	36.9%
Poor income	43.2%	38.0%	43.2%	41.2%	41.0%
IADL disability	20.3%	20.3%	20.9%	21.2%	23.4%

living arrangements except "empty-nest family with children aside". With regard to material support, significant difference was only found between respondents in skipped-generation families and those who had children close by as well as children who had migrated, with the former having more support ($p = .03$). Moreover, families with children had migrated had higher household incomes. Respondents with all children close by had significantly lower household incomes than respondents with any other living arrangements ($p < .001$).

No significant difference was found among the five living arrangements on gender, self-rated health, and IADL disability. Significant differences were reported on age ($p < .001$), education ($p < .001$), and self-rated income level ($p = .007$). Specifically, people in empty-nest families without children who had migrated were older than all the others ($p < .001$); while they had the lowest level of education, especially compared to those living with children ($p < .001$). Moreover, a significant difference was reported between empty-nest families with and without children who had migrated, with the former reporting higher incomes ($p = .011$).

Four OLS models were applied to examine the associations among living arrangements, family resources, and depression, controlling for socio-demographic variables. Utilizing "living with all children aside" as the reference group, another four living arrangement types were regressed in Model 1 on depression. In Model 2, the socio-demographic variables were controlled for. Two variables in relation to family resources were regressed in Model 3 on depression, controlling for socio-demographic variables. In Model 4, both living-arrangement type and family resources were regressed on depression, controlling for socio-demographic variables. The results are presented in Table 4.8.

Table 4.8 Regression models on depression ($N = 7,835$)

	Model 1 Coefficient	Model 2 Coefficient	Model 3 Coefficient	Model 4 Coefficient
Constant	8.84***	−6.06***	−5.01	−5.40
L1	.38	−.47*		−.66**
L2	.88***	.52**		.43*
L3	1.25***	.68*		.58*
L5	.92***	.63**		.46*
Household income			−.14***	−.15***
Material supports			.17	.19
Emotional support			−.16***	−.16***
Gender (ref.: male)		1.85***	1.77***	1.77***
Age		.07***	.05***	.06***
Education (ref.: illiterate)		−.34***	−.31***	−.31***
Self-rated income (ref.: very high)		2.42***	2.35***	2.30***
Self-rated health (ref.: excellent)		.23**	.24**	.23**
IADL disability		−.08	−.10	−.10
Adjust R²	.004	.140	.141	.144
F	9.57***	128.56***	141.91***	100.97***

Notes: * $p < .05$; ** $p < .01$; *** $p < .001$.

Model 1 showed that compared to "living with all children aside" (L4), all other living arrangements were significantly associated with higher levels of depression except for "empty-nest family without children migration" (L1). After controlling for demographic variables in Model 2, "empty-nest family with children migration" (L2), "skipped-generation family" (L3), and "living with some children aside while others migrated" (L5) were still associated with higher depression compared to L4. However, L1 turned out to be associated with significantly lower depression compared to L4 ($p < .05$). Model 3 examined the association between family resources and depression. After controlling for demographic variables, Model 3 reported that higher household income and emotional support was associated with lower depression ($p < .001$); while no significant association was found between material support and depression. Finally, Model 4 reported that after controlling for demographic variables and family resources, L2, L3, and L5 were associated with significantly higher depression compared to L4; while L1 was associated with significantly lower depression compared to L4 ($p = .003$).

4.2.4 Discussion

Many studies have discussed the effects of living arrangements on elderly mental health, while still little attention has been paid to the mental health implications of the living-arrangement shift due to the migration of the children's generation resulting from urbanization. In the context of China's urbanization, living arrangements are never a choice made by rural middle-aged and older people themselves, and the traditional Chinese family value favors co-residence or at least proximal residences among family members (Logan & Bian, 1999). Therefore, the absence of the children's generation can lead to significant negative mental health effects. This analysis has demonstrated the proposition. It is found that rural people living with all children close by reported the lowest depression; and after controlling for demographic features and family resources, this group of people still have lower depression than people with other living arrangements except the "empty-nest family without children migration". This finding has echoed past literature's emphasis on the importance of children's presence in the household (Zhang, 2004; Zunzunegui, Beland, & Otero, 2001). Moreover, it is revealed that the negative effects of the absence of the children's generation were not buffered by family resources, although there was significant association between household income and emotional support and depression. Reasons for the result could be two-fold. On the one hand, the presence of children in the household or nearby cannot be substituted by money or other material supports; while on the other hand, the available family material support for the rural mature and older population could be too limited to display sufficient buffering effects.

Another major finding is about the heterogeneity within empty-nest families. The analyses revealed that people in empty-nest families while not having children who had migrated (their children may reside in other neighborhoods of the same county or in different households of the same neighborhood) had significantly lower depression than people in all other living arrangements except "living with all children aside". And when controlling for demographic features, this group of people even reported significantly lower depression than those living with all children close by. The existing literature has reported that a moderate level of independence is beneficial to older people's mental health (Boyle, 2005; Lothian & Philp, 2001); while multi-generational households can be more often troubled by domestic conflicts (Chou & Chi, 2003; Zhan, 2004); and some older people just prefer living independently (Logan, Bian, & Bian, 1998; Zhan, 2004).

It is also worth noting the mental health vulnerability of the skipped-generation family. Faced with the double stressors, namely the absence of the children's generation and the burden of caring for grandchildren, the mature and older people in this type of family reported the highest level of depression, which still stood after the demographic features and available family resources were controlled for. On the contrary, Silverstein, Cong, and Li (2006) once reported the mental health advantage of older people in skipped-generation families in rural China, who found that receiving greater remittances from the migrated adult children increased wellbeing and explained why living with grandchildren was beneficial. The research findings can be biased since it only took monetary transfer from migrated children into account. In reality, rural families may also receive monetary and other forms of material support from family members other than children, such as parents and siblings. This study avoided the limitation by adding up material support from all family members, and no significant difference was found in the amount of family material support between the five living arrangements except between "skipped-generation family" and "living with some children aside and other children migrated". Moreover, no significant association was found between material support and depression.

4.3 Community environment restructuring and depression of Chinese rural older people

This part examines how the proxy of urbanization at the community level, namely community environment restructuring, is associated with the depression of the Chinese rural older population. Specifically, it examined whether land expropriation is associated with the depression of Chinese rural older adults, and whether the association is significantly mediated by the community physical environment and socioeconomic environment restructuring. The existing literature reveals close association between a community's socioeconomic status, the physical environment, and the depression of residents. According to Yeatts et al. (2013), environmental factors in a community, such as economic structure, grassroots organizations, leisure facilities, and basic infrastructure, can influence residents' levels of depression. Moreover, mental health interventions in the community, such as neighborhood walkability and transportation improvement, have been well recognized as effective measures to reduce residents' depression (Quijano et al., 2007). Therefore, community environment restructuring could be both a risk factor and an opportunity for depression in the older population.

According to the fundamental causes theory, the socioeconomic status of a community is closely related to the mental health of residents, since it shapes the access to resources for preventing mental problems, on the one hand, and exposure to mental health risks, on the other (Phelan, Link, & Tehranifar, 2010). This could be especially true for the aging population, whose sphere of activity may largely be confined to the residing community. Based on this ecological framework, this analysis sets out the following three research hypotheses:

(a) Land expropriation in a rural community is significantly associated with the depressive symptoms of middle-aged and older adults;
(b) The physical environment of a rural community is a significant mediator of the association between community land expropriation and the depressive symptoms of middle-aged and older adults;
(c) The socioeconomic environment of a rural community is a significant mediator of the association between community land expropriation and the depressive symptoms of the middle-aged and older adults.

This analysis involved a secondary analysis of de-identified data obtained from the Baseline of China Health and Retirement Longitudinal Study (CHALRS) project. A total of 12,628 respondents who were living in 303 rural communities were selected for research. Each community contains 12 to 86 samples. Apart from the individual-level variables, the present analysis also included the community-level data.

4.3.1 Measures

The outcome variable was depression, which was measured by using the 10-item Center for Epidemiological Studies Depression Short Form (CES-D-10). Samples responded each item from four choices (0 = "rarely or none of the time", 1 = "some or a little of the time", 2 = "occasionally or a moderate amount of the time", 3 = "most or all of the time"). The scores for the ten items were summed into a total score, with the larger value representing higher depression. The independent variable was the land expropriation status of the rural community. Like elsewhere, urban expansion-initiating community restructuring usually starts with land expropriation and change of land use in China. The variable was coded into a dummy, namely 1 represents a rural community that had land expropriated in the recent decade while 0 represents one that had not.

Five potential mediating variables were proposed, including infrastructure, recreational amenities, grassroots organization, non-agricultural industry development, and income protection scheme availability. The first two belong to the physical dimension and the remaining three belong to the socioeconomic dimension. An index summing up the availability of six infrastructure items was constructed. They included "bus service", "sewer system", "reconstructed toilet system", "tap water", "natural gas or liquefied gas", and "waste management service".

Three dichotomous variables were coded to indicate the availability of recreational amenities, grassroots organizations, and income protection schemes in the rural community. Recreational amenity items included "basketball court", "swimming pool", "outdoor fitness equipment", "table tennis", "room for card games and chess", and "room for Ping Pong". Grassroots organization items included "association for calligraphy and painting", "dancing team", "organization for helping the elderly and the handicapped", "employment services", "elderly activity center service", and "elderly association". Income protection scheme items included "minimum living allowance", "unemployment subsidy", and "pension subsidy". For these three variables respectively, communities with one or more items were coded as 1, otherwise as 0. As for non-agricultural industry development, the percentage of households engaging in non-agricultural work in the community was used as the proxy for the variable.

Four socio-demographic variables were controlled for in the analysis. They were gender (1 = male, 2 = female), age (in years), education level (1 = illiterate, 2 = elementary school or equivalent, 3 = middle school or above), and self-rated income standard (1 = very high, 2 = relatively high, 3 = average, 4 = relatively poor, 5 = poor).

4.3.2 Statistical analyses

A multilevel mediation model was constructed to analyze (1) whether there was significant correlation between community restructuring and depressive symptoms; and if yes, (2) which factor(s) were significantly mediating the correlation. Firstly, in order to necessitate the usage of multilevel modeling, the intra-class coefficient (ICC) was calculated in a null model. A community's land expropriation status and control variables were then included in the model to examine the significance of the correlation between the independent and dependent variables. Finally, the five community-level mediators were included in order to examine their significance. All statistical analyses were performed using Mplus 7.0.

4.3.3 Results

Table 4.9 shows descriptive statistics for the involved research variables. Of the 303 rural communities, 117 were found with land never having been expropriated, covering 4,628 respondents. The endorsement rate for recreational amenities, grassroots organizations, and income protection schemes in communities were 54.1%, 46.9%, and 88.1%, respectively. The percentage of households engaging in non-agricultural work and the number of infrastructure items were highly differentiated among rural communities.

Multilevel modeling results are presented in Table 4.10. Model 1 is a null model, based on which the intra-class coefficient (ICC) can be calculated, namely 5.22/(5.22+37.0) = 12.36%. It means that community-level factors explain 12.36% of the variance in depression. This necessitates the usage

Table 4.9 Descriptive statistics for research variables for the third sub-study

	Community n = 303 (%)	Individual n = 12,628 (%)	Mean	S.E.
Dependent variable				
CES-D-10 (0–30)	–	–	9.07	6.50
Independent variable				
Land expropriation (with = 1)	117 (38.6)	4,628 (36.6)	–	–
Mediating variables				
Infrastructure (0–6)	–	–	2.67	1.65
Recreational amenities (with = 1)	164 (54.1)	6,541 (51.8)	–	–
Grassroots organizations (with = 1)	142 (46.9)	5,669 (44.9)	–	–
% of household engaging in non-agricultural work (0–100%)	–	–	19.2%	0.30
Income protection schemes (with = 1)	267 (88.1)	11,056 (87.6)	–	–
Personal characteristics (control variables)				
Age (45–100)	–	–	58.99	9.80
Gender (female)	–	6,394 (50.6)	–	–
Education				
- illiterate	–	4,117 (32.6)	–	–
– elementary school or equivalent	–	5,339 (42.3)	–	–
– middle school or above	–	3,149 (24.9)	–	–
SRI*				
– very high	–	21 (.2)	–	–
– relatively high	–	298 (2.4)	–	–
– average	–	6,078 (48.1)	–	–
– relatively poor	–	3,558 (28.2)	–	–
– poor	–	1,596 (12.6)	–	–

Notes: SRI represents self-rated income standard.

of multilevel modeling. Model 2 included the socio-demographic variables, which substantially reduced AIC and BIC coefficients and improved model fit. It demonstrated that age, gender, education, and self-rated income are significant predictors ($p < .001$) for depression. That is, being younger, male, with higher education, and with higher self-rated income are significantly related with lower depressive symptoms. Model 3 included the independent variable, namely the land expropriation status of a community. It showed that people living in the communities with land expropriation had a .75-unit lower depression score ($p < .01$), controlling for the four demographic characteristics. The much smaller AIC and BIC values showed that model fit was further improved.

Table 4.11 reported the results for the multilevel mediation model. When the five proposed mediators were included in the multilevel model, the

Table 4.10 Multilevel model results for land expropriation and depressive symptoms

Fixed Effects	Model 1	Model 2	Model 3
Intercept	9.03***	8.67***	8.20***
Gender (ref.: female)	–	−1.86***	−1.86***
Age	–	.07***	.07***
Education (ref.: illiterate)			
– elementary school or equivalent	–	−1.10***	−1.10***
– middle school or above	–	−1.30***	−1.29***
SRI (ref.: poor)			
– very high	–	−7.52***	−7.56***
– relatively high	–	−6.04***	−5.99***
– average	–	−4.75***	−4.75***
– relatively poor	–	−2.56***	−2.57***
Land expropriation (ref.: without expropriation)	–	–	−.75**
Random Effects	Model 1	Model 2	Model 3
Residue	37.00***	32.40***	32.49***
Intercept	5.22***	4.06***	3.97***
Mode Fit Statistics			
AIC	70,704	68,585	68,268
BIC	70,718	68,600	68,283

Notes: *$p < .05$, **$p < .01$, ***$p < .001$.

association between land expropriation and depressive symptoms became non-significant ($p = .39$). Rural communities with land being expropriated were significantly associated with more infrastructure, recreational amenities, and grassroots organizations. However, the statistics showed that only infrastructure and grassroots organization availability were significant mediators for the association between community land expropriation status and the depressive symptoms of the rural mature and elderly population.

4.3.4 Discussion

The present analysis found that community restructuring, a result of urban expansion, has led to positive effects on the depressive symptoms of the mature and elderly population in rural China. This finding is not in line with the results of some previous studies, which reported that community restructuring was a risk factor for psychological wellbeing (Harpham & Molyneux, 2001; Yanos, 2007). The reasons for the difference can be threefold. First, urban expansion has been discussed with different discourses in the developed world and the developing world. With regard to urban expansion in developed countries, a lot of attention has been paid to urban sprawl, which implicates the development of low-density, monofunctional, and automobile-reliant communities (Couch, Leontidou, & Petschel-Held, 2007). People in these communities may be faced with consequences such

Table 4.11 Multilevel mediation modeling results

	Infrastructure	Recreational amenities	Grassroots organization	Industry development	Income protection schemes
Land expropriation (a)	.90***	.24***	.27***	.07	.04
Depression (b)	-.34***	-.28	-.63*	.20	-.29
Indirect (a*b)	-.31**	-.07	-.17*	-.01	-.01
Confidence Interval	[-.47, -.15]	[-.18, .05]	[-.32, -.03]	[-.03, .06]	[-.04, .02]

Notes: Socio-demographic features were controlled for; *p < .05, **p < .01, ***p < .001.

as longer commute times, insufficient physical activity, and lower levels of community cohesion (Costley, 2006; Soule, 2006). On the other hand, with different demographic and economic features, China and other emerging economies' urban expansion is more development-oriented, having a close association with local industry expansion, infrastructure and housing modernization, and lifestyle enrichment (Henderson, 2002). These may bring about positive effects on community dwellers' mental health.

The second reason is in relation to the different research focuses. Since urban expansion is a process of talent and capital concentration, it may attract resources from other neighboring communities and lead to their decline (Fraser et al., 2005). As a result, the mental health risks, such as fewer job opportunities and separation from family members, for the residents in communities with outflowing resources may increase. However, instead of focusing on one single type of community, this research compares communities with and without land expropriation, a form of resource reshuffling and concentration in rural China. As such, the research findings can only provide direct evidence for the gap between the two types of communities, while not for the argument that the decline of one type of community is due to resource concentration in the other type of community.

Third, the dualism in China's social structure can also contribute to the mental health advantage of residents living in a restructuring rural community. China set up the permanent household registry system (i.e., the *Hukou* system) in the 1950s, aiming to manage rural-to-urban population mobility. This system strictly categorizes Chinese people into the rural group and the urban group according to their birthplace or parents' *Hukou* status (Wang, 2005). This identity difference has significant social, political, and economic implications. Even now, China's major social welfare benefits are still allocated according to this categorization, with substantial priority given to the urban *Hukou* holders. More than half a century's persistence of the system has shaped great inequalities in socioeconomic status between rural and urban Chinese people, which can in turn lead to mental health disparities (Zimmerman & Katon, 2005). As a result of urbanization, therefore, rural community restructuring in contemporary China can be recognized by rural residents as a rare opportunity to climb the social ladder and acquire various social resources lacking in the former rural environment.

This analysis also revealed that infrastructure and grassroots organization availability in rural communities significantly mediated the association between community restructuring and depressive symptoms. Past literature has supported the positive effects of infrastructure availability on the mental health of community residents (Kirmayer, Simpson, & Cargo, 2003; Wells, Miranda, Bruce, Alegria, & Wallerstein, 2004). At the same time, community-level interventions, such as walkability and transportation enhancement schemes, were followed by increased psychological wellbeing (Leventhal & Brooks-Gunn, 2003; Sugiyama, Leslie, Giles-Corti, & Owen, 2008).

The significant mediating role of grassroots organization availability should be examined within China's historical context. Rural China was traditionally a stable acquaintance society featuring blood linkage. This was substantially changed during the political movements in the first decades after the foundation of the People's Republic of China, in which clanism and ancestral worship were overthrown by communist fever (Zhou, 1993). The spiritual commonwealth in rural China has been further weakened by the instrumentalism and economic rationality prevalent since the adoption of economic reforms in the late 1970s (Wilson, 2002). Therefore, the development of grassroots organizations for hobbies and mutual help in the process of urbanization can be a new way of organizing rural people's social and spiritual life, which in turn affects their mental health positively.

It is also worth noting that some community socioeconomic factors did not have a mediating effect on the association between land expropriation and residents' depression. This may reveal a couple of deficiencies in China's urbanization policy. On the one hand, this analysis reported that land expropriation did not lead to significantly better availability of income protection schemes. China's urbanization has long been criticized for focusing too much on the "hardware" (i.e., infrastructure) while ignoring the benefits to the affected people (Zhang & Song, 2003). In reality, land expropriation has evolved into an important source of social conflict in rural China, mainly due to the inequalities and non-transparencies in the benefit distribution process (Guo, 2001). Future policies should be more people-centered and give more consideration to the employment and income protection issues of farmers whose land is expropriated. On the other hand, this study also did not find significant association between land expropriation and the development of non-agricultural industry, meaning that a rural community with land expropriation did not see a significantly higher proportion of non-agricultural revenue than those without land expropriation. From an economic perspective, the urbanization process is accompanied by an increased share of manufacturing and service industries and a decreased share of agriculture (Moomaw & Shatter, 1996). The absence of economic structure enhancement may deteriorate the sustainability of China's urbanization.

4.4 Summary

Based on the Baseline of the CHARLS datasets, this chapter examined the influences of urbanization on the depression of the Chinese older population at the individual, household, and community levels, respectively. At the individual level, the analysis tested the associations between childhood adversity, social identity transformation in the life course (i.e., urbanization status), and the current depression situation of the Chinese rural older population. Firstly, it is reported that childhood adversity was significantly associated with the depression of Chinese rural older adults. Secondly, social identity, namely urbanization status, was significantly associated with depression. That is, urban identity was related to lower levels of depression. Thirdly, the association between childhood adversity and later-life depression was significantly moderated by identity transformation in the process of urbanization. This analysis also reveals that, as for the people with a childhood featuring low family SES and health, the higher the extent of urbanization, the higher the level of their depression. It is suggested that more social inclusive policies need to be adopted in order to guarantee the equal distribution of wellbeing led by urbanization.

At the household level, this research tested two study hypotheses. First, living with children close by was associated with lower level of depression, and this was especially true for those living independently while all children were living close by. Second, the family resources, including household income, material support from family members, and emotional support from children, could not compensate for the negative effects resulting from the out-migration of the children's generation for the Chinese rural older population. It is also suggested that special attention should be paid to the mental health of aging people in the skipped-generation families.

At the community level, this analysis examined three research hypotheses. First, land expropriation in Chinese rural community was significantly associated with the depression of the rural older residents, with the residents in restructuring communities reporting a .75-unit lower depression score ($p < .01$). Second, with regard to the physical environment of a rural community, the degree of infrastructure was a significant mediator of the association between community land expropriation and the depressive symptoms of the middle-aged and older residents ($p < .01$); while no significant indirect effect was found on availability of recreational amenities. Third, with regard to the socioeconomic environment of a rural community, availability of grassroots organizations is a significant mediator of the association between community land expropriation and the depression of the rural older residents ($p < .05$); while no significant indirect effect was found on non-agricultural industry development and availability of income protection schemes.

The findings of this study add to an understanding of the relationship between community restructuring and depressive symptoms in the context of urbanization. It may also generate important policy implications that are not only applicable in China, but also in other developing countries. That is, an urbanization policy should focus on not only the reshaping of the physical environment in rural community, but also the development of grassroots organizations that involve local people, the upgrading of local economic structures, and the establishment of income protection and other welfare arrangements for affected people.

References

Barker, D. J. (1997). Maternal nutrition, fetal nutrition, and disease in later life. *Nutrition, 13*(9), 807–813. doi:10.1016/S0899-9007(97)00193-7

Beard, J. R., & Petitot, C. (2010). Aging and urbanization: Can cities be designed to foster active aging. *Public Health Reviews, 32*(2), 427–450.

Björgvinsson, T., Kertz, S. J., Bigda-Peyton, J. S., McCoy, K. L., & Aderka, I. M. (2013). Psychometric properties of the CES-D-10 in a psychiatric sample. *Assessment, 20*(4), 429–436.

Blazer, D. G. (2003). Depression in late life: Review and commentary. *The Journals of Gerontology Series A: Biological Sciences and Medical Sciences, 58*(3), M249–M265.

Boyle, G. (2005). The role of autonomy in explaining mental ill-health and depression among older people in long-term care settings. *Aging and Society, 25*(5), 731–748. doi:10.1017/S0144686X05003703

Bradley, R. H., & Corwyn, R. F. (2002). Socioeconomic status and child development. *Annual Review of Psychology, 53*(1), 371–399. doi:10.1146/annurev.psych.53.100901.135233

Brown, D. L., Cromartie, J. B., & Kulcsar, L. J. (2004). Micropolitan areas and the measurement of American urbanization. *Population Research and Policy Review, 23*(4), 399–418. doi:10.1023/B:POPU.0000040044.72272.16

Charles, S. T., Reynolds, C. A., & Gatz, M. (2001). Age-related differences and change in positive and negative affect over 23 years. *Journal of Personality and Social Psychology, 80*(1), 136. doi:10.1037/0022-3514.80.1.136

Chen, X. (1985). The one-child population policy, modernization, and the extended Chinese family. *Journal of Marriage and the Family, 47*(1), 193–202. doi:10.2307/352082

Chen, Y., & Zhou, L.-A. (2007). The long-term health and economic consequences of the 1959–1961 famine in China. *Journal of Health Economics, 26*(4), 659–681. doi:10.1016/j.jhealeco.2006.12.006

Chou, K.-L., & Chi, I. (2003). Reciprocal relationship between social support and depressive symptoms among Chinese elderly. *Aging & Mental Health, 7*(3), 224–231. doi:10.1080/136031000101210

Costley, D. (2006). Master planned communities: Do they offer a solution to urban sprawl or a vehicle for seclusion of the more affluent consumers in Australia? *Housing, Theory and Society, 23*(3), 157–175.

Couch, C., Leontidou, L., & Petschel-Held, G. (2007). *Urban Sprawl in Europe.* Hoboken, NJ: Wiley.

Djernes, J. (2006). Prevalence and predictors of depression in populations of elderly: A review. *Acta Psychiatrica Scandinavica, 113*(5), 372–387. Retrieved from http://onlinelibrary.wiley.com/store/10.1111/j.1600-0447.2006.00770.x/ asset/j.1600-0447.2006.00770.x.pdf?v=1&t=i1g3f4bt&s=19a3f108bf070b94f8 7d988f12e239eaaaac2797.

Elder Jr, G. H. (1999). *Children of the Great Depression: Social Change in Life Experience*. Boulder, CO: Westview Press.

Fergusson, D. M., & Horwood, L. J. (2003). Resilience to childhood adversity: Results of a 21-year study. In S. S. Luthar (Ed.), *Resilience and Vulnerability: Adaptation in the Context of Childhood Adversities* (pp. 130–155). Cambridge: Cambridge University Press.

Field, A. (2009). *Discovering Statistics Using SPSS*. London: Sage.

Fraser, C., Jackson, H., Judd, F., Komiti, A., Robins, G., Murray, G., … Hodgins, G. (2005). Changing places: The impact of rural restructuring on mental health in Australia. *Health & Place, 11*(2), 157–171.

Gørgens, T., Meng, X., & Vaithianathan, R. (2012). Stunting and selection effects of famine: A case study of the Great Chinese Famine. *Journal of Development Economics, 97*(1), 99–111.

Guo, X. (2001). Land expropriation and rural conflicts in China. *The China Quarterly, 166*, 422–439.

Harpham, T., & Molyneux, C. (2001). Urban health in developing countries: A review. *Progress in Development Studies, 1*(2), 113–137.

Henderson, V. (2002). Urbanization in developing countries. *The World Bank Research Observer, 17*(1), 89–112.

Kirmayer, L., Simpson, C., & Cargo, M. (2003). Healing traditions: Culture, community and mental health promotion with Canadian Aboriginal peoples. *Australasian Psychiatry, 11*(s1), S15–S23. doi:10.1046/j.1038-5282.2003.02010.x

Leung, J. C. (2006). The emergence of social assistance in China. *International Journal of Social Welfare, 15*(3), 188–198. doi:10.1111/j.1468-2397.2006.00434.x

Leventhal, T., & Brooks-Gunn, J. (2003). Moving to opportunity: An experimental study of neighborhood effects on mental health. *American Journal of Public Health, 93*(9), 1576–1582.

Li, W. (1994). *The Top Ten Famines in Modern China*. Shanghai: Shanghai People's Publishing House.

Logan, J. R., & Bian, F. (1999). Family values and coresidence with married children in urban China. *Social Forces, 77*(4), 1253–1282. doi:10.2307/3005876

Logan, J. R., Bian, F., & Bian, Y. (1998). Tradition and change in the urban Chinese family: The case of living arrangements. *Social Forces, 76*(3), 851–882. doi:10.1093/sf/76.3.851

Lothian, K., & Philp, I. (2001). Care of older people: Maintaining the dignity and autonomy of older people in the healthcare setting. *BMJ: British Medical Journal, 322*(7287), 668.

Luppa, M., Sikorski, C., Luck, T., Ehreke, L., Konnopka, A., Wiese, B., … Riedel-Heller, S. (2012). Age-and gender-specific prevalence of depression in latest-life: Systematic review and meta-analysis. *Journal of Affective Disorders, 136*(3), 212–221.

Martin, P., & Martin, M. (2002). Proximal and distal influences on development: The model of developmental adaptation. *Developmental Review, 22*(1), 78–96.

Moomaw, R. L., & Shatter, A. M. (1996). Urbanization and economic development: A bias toward large cities? *Journal of Urban Economics, 40*(1), 13–37. doi:10.1006/juec.1996.0021

Nylund, K. L., Asparouhov, T., & Muthén, B. O. (2007). Deciding on the number of classes in latent class analysis and growth mixture modeling: A Monte Carlo simulation study. *Structural Equation Modeling, 14*(4), 535–569. doi:10.1080/10705510701575396

Ou, M.-H., Li, W.-Y., Liu, X.-N., & Chen, M. (2004). Comprehensive measurement of district's urbanization level: A case study of Jiangsu Province. *Resources and Environment in the Yangtze Basin, 13*(5), 407–412.

Phelan, J. C., Link, B. G., & Tehranifar, P. (2010). Social conditions as fundamental causes of health inequalities theory, evidence, and policy implications. *Journal of Health and Social Behavior, 51*(1 suppl), S28–S40. doi:10.1177/0022146510383498

Piccinelli, M., & Wilkinson, G. (2000). Gender differences in depression: Critical review. *British Journal of Psychiatry, 177*, 486–492. Retrieved from <Go to ISI>://WOS:000165851200003. http://bjp.rcpsych.org/content/177/6/486.full.pdf. doi:10.1192/bjp.177.6.486

Quijano, L. M., Stanley, M. A., Petersen, N. J., Casado, B. L., Steinberg, E. H., Cully, J. A., & Wilson, N. L. (2007). Healthy IDEAS a depression intervention delivered by community-based case managers serving older adults. *Journal of Applied Gerontology, 26*(2), 139–156.

Silverstein, M., Cong, Z., & Li, S. (2006). Intergenerational transfers and living arrangements of older people in rural China: Consequences for psychological well-being. *The Journals of Gerontology Series B: Psychological Sciences and Social Sciences, 61*(5), S256–S266.

Sonnenberg, C. M., Beekman, A. T., Deeg, D. J., & Tilburg, W. v. (2000). Sex differences in late-life depression. *Acta Psychiatrica Scandinavica, 101*(4), 286–292. doi:10.1034/j.1600-0447.2000.101004286.x

Soule, D. C. (2006). *Urban Sprawl: A Comprehensive Reference Guide.* Santa Barbara, CA: Greenwood Publishing Group.

Sugiyama, T., Leslie, E., Giles-Corti, B., & Owen, N. (2008). Associations of neighbourhood greenness with physical and mental health: Do walking, social coherence and local social interaction explain the relationships? *Journal of Epidemiology and Community Health, 62*(5), e9–e9.

Wainwright, N., & Surtees, P. (2002). Childhood adversity, gender and depression over the life-course. *Journal of Affective Disorders, 72*(1), 33–44. doi:10.1016/S0165-0327(01)00420-7

Wang, C. (2001). Social identity of the new generation of rural hobo and merger of urban and rural. *Sociological Research,* (3), 63–76.

Wang, C. (2006). A study of floating rural people's "semi-urbanization" (in Chinese). *Sociological Studies, 5*(7), 107–122.

Wang, F. (2005). *Organizing through Division and Exclusion: China's Hukou System.* Stanford, CA: Stanford University Press.

Wells, K., Miranda, J., Bruce, M. L., Alegria, M., & Wallerstein, N. (2004). Bridging community intervention and mental health services research. *American Journal of Psychiatry, 161*(6), 955–963. doi:10.1176/appi.ajp.161.6.955

Werner, E. E., & Smith, R. S. (2001). *Journeys from Childhood to Midlife: Risk, Resilience, and Recovery.* Ithaca, NY: Cornell University Press.

Wilson, L. B. (2006). *Civic Engagement and the Baby Boomer Generation: Research, Policy, and Practice Perspectives.* London: Psychology Press.

Wilson, S. (2002). Face, norms, and instrumentality. In T. Gold, D. Guthrie, & D. Wank (Eds.), *Social Connections in China* (pp. 163–178). Cambridge: Cambridge University Press.

Yanos, P. T. (2007). Beyond "Landscapes of Despair": The need for new research on the urban environment, sprawl, and the community integration of persons with severe mental illness. *Health & Place, 13*(3), 672–676.

Yeatts, D. E., Pei, X., Cready, C. M., Shen, Y., Luo, H., & Tan, J. (2013). Village characteristics and health of rural Chinese older adults: Examining the CHARLS pilot study of a rich and poor province. *Social Science & Medicine, 98*, 71–78.

Zeng, Y. (1986). Changes in family structure in China: A simulation study. *Population and Development Review, 12*(4), 675–703. doi:10.2307/1973431

Zhan, H. J. (2004). Willingness and expectations: Intergenerational differences in attitudes toward filial responsibility in China. *Marriage & Family Review, 36*(1–2), 175–200. doi:10.1300/J002v36n01_08

Zhang, F. Q. (2004). Economic transition and new patterns of parent-adult child coresidence in Urban China. *Journal of Marriage and Family, 66*(5), 1231–1245. doi:10.1111/j.0022-2445.2004.00089.x

Zhang, K. H., & Song, S. (2003). Rural–urban migration and urbanization in China: Evidence from time-series and cross-section analyses. *China Economic Review, 14*(4), 386–400.

Zhou, X. (1993). Unorganized interests and collective action in communist China. *American Sociological Review, 58*(1), 54–73.

Zimmerman, F. J., & Katon, W. (2005). Socioeconomic status, depression disparities, and financial strain: What lies behind the income-depression relationship? *Health Economics, 14*(12), 1197–1215. doi:10.1002/hec.1011

Zunzunegui, M. V., Beland, F., & Otero, A. (2001). Support from children, living arrangements, self-rated health and depressive symptoms of older people in Spain. *International Journal of Epidemiology, 30*(5), 1090–1099. doi:10.1093/ije/30.5.1090

5 Localization of foreign community-based care models in urbanizing China

5.1 Localization of the Program of All-Inclusive Care for the Elderly (PACE)

The Program of All-Inclusive Care for the Elderly (PACE) is a Medicare program targeting people who are aged 55 or above and eligible to receive nursing home care but are able to live safely in community settings. According to the National PACE Association (2018), there were 124 PACE organizations in 31 US states serving more than 45,000 participants as of January 2018, and the enrollment has more than doubled from under 20,000 participants in 2011. It is reported that over 40% of PACE participants were diagnosed as having serious mental illness (SMI), including major depressive disorder and bipolar affective disorder, and the number of participants with SMI is increasing (National PACE Association, 2014). Therefore, mental health care is an important part of the services provided by PACE organizations, although these organizations are not required by the Centers for Medicare & Medicaid Services to include mental health and psychiatric specialists on the interdisciplinary care team (Ginsburg & Eng, 2009).

PACE has two major components, namely (1) an adult day health center where services are provided; and (2) an interdisciplinary care team comprising the necessary members, including a primary care provider, a registered nurse, a master's level social worker, a home-care coordinator, physical and occupational therapists, a dietitian, and others. Specifically, services for older participants with serious mental illness include five aims: (1) design participant assessment processes that identify and immediately support complex needs; (2) align interdisciplinary care team roles to meet the needs of older adults with serious mental illness; (3) prioritize training during implementation of new behavioral health models of care and for continuous improvement; (4) create a therapeutic environment to meet participants needs; and (5) create collaborative partnerships by contracting with external providers.

DOI: 10.4324/9781003248767-5

5.1.1 China's version of PACE: Comprehensive Services Center for the Elderly

As an important measure to deal with population aging, Shanghai initiated the program of establishing a Comprehensive Services Center for the Elderly (CSCE) in every subdistrict and township since 2013. Together with other urban planning and community renewal programs, CSCE is aimed at creating a hub-like service complex for the community-dwelling older people, providing them with instrumental care, rehabilitation care, spiritual comfort, cultural entertainment, emergency assistance, and other convenient and accessible "one-stop" services. This program has significantly changed Shanghai's community-based care services, which were troubled by fragmented resources as well as inaccurate targeting.

The CSCE program is guaranteed by an amount of local legislation. In March 2016, the Shanghai Municipal Office on Population Aging issued the "*Instructions on Strengthening the Construction of Comprehensive Service Centers for the Elderly*". The document proposes that CSCEs should adhere to the principle of being people-centered and demand-oriented, enabling older people to live in a familiar environment and enhancing their sense of community and happiness, through strengthening management and optimizing services. In 2017, the General Office of the Municipal Government forwarded the "*Measures for the Management of Shanghai Community Elderly Care Services*" formulated by the Civil Affairs Bureau, again clarifying that all subdistricts and township governments should carry out a CSCE building program. It is required that newly built CSCEs should play a pivotal role in integrating long-term care resources, improving the community elderly care service network, promoting the linkage between demands and services, and enhancing the comprehensive management standard of elderly care services.

According to the 13th Five-Year Plan on Population Aging Affairs of Shanghai, CSCE would be an integral part of the municipality's framework for developing its elderly care services, namely the "Five Circles" Project. The plan stated that Shanghai will construct community-based facilities for elderly care according to older people's life radiuses, forming a facility network covering both urban and rural areas that features "Five Circles" and "one center, multiple branches". The first circle is the comprehensive service circle within each subdistrict. CSCE is established in each subdistrict across Shanghai, with the aim of integrating and coordinating elderly care facilities within the region and providing one-stop services for older people based on an information-management platform. The second is the community institutional-care service circle. Shanghai is making efforts to build more day-care centers and community-based long-term care service centers, aiming at strengthening service provision for the disabled, older people living with dementia, and the oldest of the old (namely people aged 80 or above). At the same time, this circle is also supposed to facilitate the integration of medical treatment and long-term care, the upgrading of the community canteen services, and the expansion of the policy coverage. The third is the activity circle, which requires the establishment of at least one standardized activity room for the elderly in every neighborhood committee or village. The fourth is the neighborhood mutual support circle, which encourages the construction of community mutual support facilities in villages and neighborhoods utilizing residents' underused houses, aiming for the promotion of the mutual-support elderly care model. The fifth is the home life circle, which aims to build a secure and accessible living environment for older people, through renovating staircases, putting public facilities into communities, and living spaces to cater for older people's needs.

The CSCE is positioned as the pivot among the five circles. By the middle of 2020, 268 CSCEs had been established in Shanghai, realizing the goal of building one CSCE in every township or subdistrict a year in advance (Jiang, 2020). The responsibilities of CSCE are four-fold. First, it provides a "one-stop service" for all community-dwelling older people, including community-based long-term care services, medical treatment and instrumental care services, daily life assistance, and supporting services for aging at home. Second, the organization utilizes various types of service resources for the elderly to achieve "integrated resource pooling". Subdistrict and township governments are supposed to give full play to the pivotal role of this comprehensive public service platform, focusing on the overall planning of administrative resources, social resources, and market resources to maximize service benefits. The third responsibility is to establish a platform that assists older people's daily lives with science and technology, achieving the goal of "managing service information by one network". CSCE's daily operation is based on information technology, which is developed under the framework of "two levels of platform" (i.e., municipality- and district-level platforms) and "three levels of network" (i.e., municipality-, district-, and subdistrict-level networks). The fourth major responsibility is to provide accessible public services to community-dwelling older people and their family members.

5.2 Localization of the time bank solution

In his book *Time Dollars: The New Currency that Enables Americans to Turn Their Hidden Resources – Time – Into Personal Security and Community Renewal*, attorney Edgar Cahn coined the term "Time Dollar". After writing this book in 1992, he further coined the terms "TimeBank" and "Time

Credit". According to him, the fast growth of time bank in the United States was because the financial support of social programs had declined while no alternatives had been proposed to deal with the situation. He later claimed that contemporary American society was faced with three major interconnected problems, namely (1) the widening gap between the rich and the poor and the poor is creating less and less access to the most basic services and commodities; (2) increased social problems as a result of dissolving families and communities; and (3) increasing dissatisfaction toward the failures of community renewal and public programs that aim to address the above problems. Attorney Cahn paid special attention to the top-down attitudes in delivering social services, and he believed that a major drawback of many social services organizations is that the people they are trying to help do not want help. He called this a deficit-based approach of delivering social services, through which organizations identify needs and focus on problems. Rather, he proposed, an asset-based approach should be adopted, to which every person in the community can make contributions. A model such as time bank follows this approach and can rebuild an infrastructure of trust and compassion and strengthen families and communities (Valek & Bures, 2018). In his book, attorney Cahn hoped that time bank could make individuals and communities more self-sufficient, avoiding the unpredictable influences of politics (Cahn & Rowe, 1992).

Time bank is a tool for community development, which provides a hotbed for talent and an experience exchange within a community. It strengthens family and community by assessing and awarding mutual help. The first time bank in the world was established by Teruko Mizushima in Japan in 1973. She saw time as constituting an alternative form of trade to money. She based her bank on the simple concept that each hour of time given as a service to others could earn reciprocal hours of service for the giver at some stage in the future. She envisaged that individuals could contribute time when their lives were less busy and draw down on this later when necessary. In this way, depositors could make more effective use of time across their life course and could receive help when they needed it in old age. Mizushima thus looked to deal with the problems of an aging society long before these became apparent. Later in the 1990s, attorney Cahn initiated this movement in the United States, and Martin Simon also started exploration in the UK.

Paul Glover invented Ithaca Hours in 1991. The value of each hour of Ithaca is 1 basic labor hour or $10.00. Professionals have the right to charge multiple Ithaca Hours per hour, but usually they lower their rates in a spirit of fairness. Millions of dollars' worth of Ithaca Hours are traded among thousands of residents and 500 businesses, providing interest-free Ithaca-hour loans and Ithaca-hour subsidies to more than 100 community organizations (Collom, 2005). In 2017, Nimses introduced the concept "nim", a time-based currency. 1 nim = 1 minute of life time. This concept was first adopted in Eastern Europe. The concept is based on the concept of universal basic income. Everyone is an issuer of nims. For every minute of one's life, one creates a nim that can be spent or given to others (Nejati, Salamzadeh, & Salamzadeh, 2011).

As a philosophy, time bank bases trade on five principles (Cahn & Rowe, 1992), or core values, namely: (1) everyone is an asset and society's real wealth is its people; (2) some work is beyond pricing, and work has to be redefined to value whatever it takes to raise healthy children, build strong families, revitalize neighborhoods, advance social justice, and make the planet sustainable; (3) reciprocity – we should ask: "How can we help each other build the world we both will live in?"; (4) networks are stronger than individuals, that is, people helping each other reweave communities of support, strength, and trust; and (5) every human being matters, and we must respect where people are in the moment, not where we hope they will be at some future point.

5.2.1 China's explorations of the time bank model

It is commonly recognized that the first time bank in China was established in the Jinyang Neighborhood Committee of Tilanqiao Subdistrict, Hongkou District, Shanghai, in 1998. Since then, this model has been promoted in many cities across the country. According to the classification of Chen and Huang (2017), the development process of time bank in China can be roughly divided into three stages. The first stage is between 1998 and 2003, when the main form of time banking was that neighborhood committee mobilized the young-olds in the community to provide services for the old-olds and used the timebook to record the service time and service content, so that the former could exchange services in the future. Since its initiation in Shanghai, government officials and civic organizations from all over the country had come to see it and had taken the model back home. Within a few years, time banks appeared in Taiyuan, Guangzhou, Beijing, Nanjing, Hangzhou, Harbin, and other cities, and some of them are still in operation. The second stage was between 2003 and 2008, when the development of time banks stagnated. Due to the lack of proper conversion standards for different services, an insufficient number of participants, and high demand by the elderly along with low provision of the services, most of the time banks were closed down. In the third stage, time banks witnessed rapid growth. Due to the occurrence of public events such as the Beijing Olympic Games and the Wenchuan earthquake, the spirit of volunteering in the whole of society greatly increased, and time bank regained public attention. It is also noted that the development of time bank in this stage is no longer solely dominated by the government; three different models emerged and thrived (Li & Cao, 2019).

The first model is the time bank spontaneously established by the community, which is the major type in China's explorations of time banking. Typical cases include the Jinyang Time Bank in Shanghai, namely the first time bank in China, and the Zhaoyuan Community Time Bank in Nanjing. This type of time bank has the following characteristics: (1) early development; (2) initiated by the community neighborhood committee; (3) the neighborhood committee cadres take the lead to participate; and (4) the scope of service is limited to the community residents. For instance, the Jinyang Time Bank was initiated by the Jinyang Neighborhood Committee, and the secretary of the neighborhood committee took the lead in participating in the time bank to encourage community residents to follow; and the Zhaoyuan Time Bank was initiated by the director of the neighborhood committee. Their services were only provided to local residents, due to the limitation of resources and organizations' managing scope. Moreover, as an affiliate of the community neighborhood committee, time bank is operated by members of the neighborhood committee. The dual identity of staff somewhat facilitates the promotion of time bank in the community, while it also means that the staff are not professional and are unable to devote themselves fully to the further development of the organization. This model also has the problem of inadequate use of information technology. Since this model confines its services only to community residents, there is not a strong demand for information technology, and the records of services and exchanges are mainly based on traditional paperwork. In fact, the inconvenience and insecurity of information preservation was the key reason for the collapse of the Jinyang Time Bank. It is also worth noting that this model makes preliminary explorations for the operation and regulations of time bank in China, which provides real-life experience and lessons for later practices.

The second model is the time bank co-founded by the community and enterprises or civic organizations. Typical cases include the time bank co-sponsored by Fortune 9 E-Commerce Company and the community neighborhood committee in Shanghai, the time bank based in community health service center in Shigu District of Hengyang City, and the time bank of Bayonglou Community in Zhejiang Province's Jinhua City that cooperates with the social work service center established by teachers and students of Zhejiang Normal University. The most significant feature of this model lies in its association with the market or the third sector. For example, as the largest home-care services provider of China, Fortune No. 9's cooperation with the community has created an O2O model, which links the online and offline: as with the online part, an IT platform is established and service participants can either select tasks or announce needs, as well as record the receipts and disbursements of the time currency; while for the offline part, more than 3,000 home-care service stores can deliver services to the empty-nesters located in hundreds of urban communities across the country. The time bank in Shigu District of Hengyang City, together with the School of Nursing in the University of South China, formed a model featuring a combination of medical treatment and daily care. The Ba Yonglou community's time bank takes advantage of the expertise of professional social workers, forming a linkage mechanism through civic organization cultivation, social worker participation, and community building.

The third model is the time bank established according to government programs of procuring public services from nongovernmental sectors. Due to government promotion, the numbers of these types of time bank are steadily increasing, though currently they are still uncommon. A typical case of this model is the time bank in Nansha District of Guangzhou, which has the following two characteristics. The first is that the government has a strong presence in the operation process. This, on the one hand, guarantees financial sustainability for the organization; while on the other hand, with the endorsement of government, community residents are more likely to trust the organization and thus participate in the time bank activities. For instance, the Nansha Time Bank had established a branch in every township of the district within a short period since June 2017. The second characteristic is about its clearly defined development goal. Usually, this time bank model has to set clear quantitative goals in exchange for the government's continuous financial support. This, at the same time, provides systematic standards for performance evaluation.

5.3 Localization of the gatekeeper training for suicide prevention

The mental health gatekeeper model started in Philadelphia, USA in the 1860s. It was originally designed to train "people in the community who have daily face-to-face contact with most community members" to identify people at risk of suicide in the community and provide referrals, treatment, or appropriate support services (Burnette, Ramchand, & Ayer, 2015).

In its subsequent development, this model has continuously expanded its application scenarios and has been used in education, medical care, and the military. In view of the fact that the mental health problems of the elderly in China's vast rural areas are widespread, mainly due to the outmigration of rural young labors and to their financial difficulties, the Medical Sociology Center and Public Health Research Center of Tsinghua University started a project called "Chinese Rural Elderly Community Action Plan for Psychological Crisis Intervention" since 2011. As of 2015, three phases of the project had been accomplished, including project promotion, piloting, and county sample selection. During the process, the researchers completed the intervention study on 992 elderly people in 11 villages and the control study on 1,035 elderly people in another 11 villages. These 22 villages are located in 7 provinces across China, including Heilongjiang, Inner Mongolia, Shandong, Yunnan, Sichuan, Guangxi and Fujian. The fourth phase of the project, which started in 2015, involved 8 intervention villages (with a sample size of 798 participants) and 8 control villages (with a sample size of 877 participants). Apart from the five provinces mentioned above, namely Heilongjiang, Inner Mongolia, Shandong, Yunnan, and Sichuan, three new project sites in Henan, Gansu, and Anhui were added. It is on the basis of these investigations and studies that the project team has concluded a set of social intervention models for the mental health of the elderly in rural communities with the Gatekeeper Program as the core. This model is closely integrated with local reality, has a solid research foundation, diverse forms of activities, flexible and effective multi-sectoral cooperation mechanisms, and the use of multi-dimensional social intervention measures. Overall, it has achieved remarkable results and is widely recognized in the region, and is especially welcomed by the elderly in rural communities.

5.3.1 The "Psychological Crisis Intervention Program for the Elderly in Rural China" project

The "Psychological Crisis Intervention for the Elderly in Rural China" project has a relatively solid research foundation, which is mainly reflected in the following four aspects, namely: a mature theoretical framework, strong organizational capabilities, a rigorous survey process, and deep recognition from the participants. First of all, in terms of theoretical framework, the project promotes and relies on voluntary services, which is the spirit of reciprocity and mutual assistance in rural communities. This spirit has long existed in rural society in China. According to Dr. Fei Xiaotong's formulation, in rural China the relationship between people in traditional Chinese society is based on blood and geography, and the extent of intimacy shrinks from core family to clan, to in-laws, and to neighbors (Fei, 1992). Specifically, there are various forms of mutual assistance, and they exist widely in rural areas across the country. Sociologists mostly explain the widespread existence of this spirit in China's rural areas from the functionalism perspective and the moralism perspective. The most direct manifestation of this spirit in the life of the rural elderly is the emergence of various models of mutual assistance for the elderly. In ancient times, there were mutual aid organizations such as

"Yi Zhuang" and "Aunty House"; now there are also rural elderly associations and other mutual assistance models for the elderly.

Secondly, in terms of organizational capability, the project designed a three-level pyramid structure to implement intervention plans. At the top of the pyramid is a cooperative group composed of officials from local government bodies and experts in the field of mental health. These officials mostly come from local women's federations, family planning agencies, and centers for disease control (CDCs), who are responsible for project organization and coordination, such as finding experts, organizing gatekeeper training, and promoting multi-sectoral cooperation; experts include qualified psychological counselors and psychiatrists, who are responsible for supervising psychological screening at the village level, using professional knowledge to provide education, training, and necessary mental health interventions. If they encounter unsolvable problems, they will refer the elderly to the local psychiatric hospital or other general hospitals' psychiatric departments. The middle layer of the pyramid is composed of officials from the township government, such as the cadres of the township family planning department and the women's federation. They play the mediator role in the project, and their level of cooperation is crucial to the implementation of the entire project. The bottom layer of the pyramid is the village cadres, group leaders, village women directors, village doctors, and school teachers. These people play the specific role of "gatekeeper" and are the core of the entire project. Most of them were between 40 and 60 years old. Because they live in the village all year round and have frequent contact with the villagers in their daily work, they have a better understanding of the situations of the elderly in the village and have certain prestige and service capabilities. The tasks they undertook in the project include: carrying out psychological screening, providing assistance for organizing mental health education, monitoring the mental state of the elderly, regularly organizing collective activities (such as square dancing), and referral of high-risk groups to psychiatric department doctors and other specialist offices.

Third, this project has a rigorous and scientific investigation basis, and the intervention subjects are classified according to the investigation results. The baseline survey of the project is divided into three steps: (1) preliminary communication; (2) selection and training of investigators; (3) determination of sampling methods and survey samples. In the specific sampling process, 100 elderly people aged 60 and above were randomly selected from each selected village as the survey samples. The project also established an evaluation principle with a questionnaire survey as the core and a combination of qualitative evaluation and expert evaluation.

Specifically, in the questionnaire survey, they designed a questionnaire called "Chinese Elderly Emotional Problem Intervention Demonstration

Research Questionnaire-Rural Elderly Emotional Health Evaluation". The main content is divided into two sections, namely the socio-demographic information section and the psychological problems screening tools section. In the psychological problems screening section, the scales used include: "Center of Epidemiological Studies – Depression" (CES-D, with 20 questions), "UCLA Loneliness Scale" (ULS-8, with 9 questions), "Inventory of Activities of Daily Living Ability" (ADL, with 14 questions), "Life Event Scale for the Elderly" (with 38 questions), "Quality of Life Scale" (QOL, with 6 questions), "Social Support Rating Scale" (with 11 questions), "Depression Screening Scale" (with 16 questions), "Alcohol Use Disorder Screening Scale" (AUDIT) (with 10 questions), and "Suicidal Ideation, Plan, Posture, Attempt Scale" (with 5 questions). The qualitative assessment part includes randomly selecting a number of empty-nest elderly, family members of the elderly, village committee cadres, and gatekeepers, using paired case interviews and semi-structured interviews to conduct qualitative comparative analysis. In the expert evaluation section, the project established an expert evaluation and supervision team composed of sociology experts, gerontologists, psychologists, psychiatrists, social policy researchers, social work scholars, and other professionals.

According to the questionnaire survey, the project team found that mental health problems such as loneliness, anxiety, and depression exist to varying degrees in rural elderly groups in China. There are five main influencing factors. The first is high economic pressure. There are two main reasons for this. One is that both the elderly and their children have low economic incomes; and the second is that although some of the children have the ability to support the elderly, they refuse to do so. The second influencing factor is about conflicts within the family, such as conflicts between mother-in-law and daughter-in-law and abdication of the responsibilities to care for the elderly. The third factor influencing mental health is chronic illness among the elderly. It is a common situation that chronic diseases are accompanied by depression. The fourth influencing factor is the lack of entertainment activities and spiritual comfort. The last factor is the lack of knowledge and information related to mental health. Based on these data, the project team divided the rural elderly who participated in the study into three categories: the no intervention group, the group on the verge of intervention (risk population), and the group needing referral services (high-risk population). This classification was mainly based on CES-D scores. That is, participants with a CES-D score <16 would fall into the no intervention group; those with a CES-D score > 16 while having no suicidal ideation or behaviors in the past 12 months would fall into the group on the verge of intervention; and those with a CES-D score > 16 and with suicidal ideation or behaviors in the past 12 months would fall into the group needing referral services.

Fourth, the project won deep recognition from the participants. Due to the establishment of the "gatekeeper" project, the rural elderly people involved gained increasing communication and interaction opportunities, which helped them get out of their households and interact and help each other. In addition, due to the decline of the rural collective economy and the vast outmigration of young and middle-aged laborers from the rural areas, many rural elderly people suffered from long-term ignorance and chronic loneliness, and they regard this intervention plan as concern and warmth from the state. At the same time, the selected "gatekeepers" of the project were also very cooperative. They held the belief that caring for the elderly today is to care for themselves who will become old in the future, that is, "giving someone a rose will give you a lingering fragrance".

Finally, as with the forms of activity, the project implemented four major types of activities. The first is to provide necessary training sessions to the gatekeepers, such as participating in mental health education programs, training seminars and demonstrations, and lectures on the common causes of psychological crises and suicidal behaviors. The second is to build a platform to establish a registration system for mutual contact between the gatekeeper and the elderly in the group, and to make and issue a "contact card for help"; at the same time, it also established a channel for the gatekeeper to contact a psychiatrist or expert to ensure that each gatekeeper can implement the referral service. The third is to establish a record system for the gatekeeper's random visits to the older people in the no intervention group, as well as a record system for regular visits to the at-risk and high-risk groups. Each visit by the gatekeeper should last at least 30 minutes, and the content of the visit may include:

- Explaining to the older people one by one, using the mental health literacies stated in the specifically designed brochures;
- Bringing some knowledge and information related to physical and mental health each time;
- Telling older people that they can contact the gatekeepers when faced with any kind of health problems;
- Writing the "Gatekeeper's Diary".

The fourth type of activity is that the gatekeeper divided the older people on the verge of intervention into subgroups comprised of 4 to 5 members, according to similarities in demographics. Regular activities would be organized to encourage the elderly to interact and help each other.

During the implementation of the project, in close collaboration with the local committees on population aging and charity associations, a wide range of activities to care for the elderly in rural areas are carried out. In the operation process, the responsibilities and cooperation division of each department are as follows:

- Committee on Population Aging: coordinate and promote various departments and units to strengthen the guidance and management of elderly care related affairs, and carry out activities that are beneficial to the physical and mental health of the elderly; guide, supervise, and inspect the elderly care related affairs of various towns, subdistricts, and villages; organize and coordinate related significant events of elderly care related affairs;
- Civilization Office: shape a more friendly social environment for the elderly and protect the legitimate rights and interests of the elderly;
- Bureau of Civil Affairs: formulate plans for the development of elderly care services, develop elderly care projects, and play a leading role in the construction and management of elderly care services and facilities; formulate social support policies for the elderly; implement the rural "five guarantees" policies (guarantee basic food, clothing, medical services, shelter, and place of burial) and strengthen the construction of rural nursing homes; provide support and assistance to the elderly living below the poverty line;
- Bureau of Culture, Broadcasting and News: researching and formulating the development plan of the cultural and entertainment activities for the elderly and the implementation of the plan; organization of older people oriented cultural activities; giving support to the making of excellent cultural works that shape a friendly and respectful social environment for the elderly; supporting the construction of entertainment venues for the elderly;
- Healthcare Commission: to study, formulate, and organize the implementation of medical and health care plans for the elderly; improve the medical and health care service network for the elderly; play a leading role in the prevention, treatment, health care, and rehabilitation of geriatric diseases, and provide high-quality, efficient and convenient medical and health services for elderly patients;
- Bureau of Justice: stress laws and regulations on older people's rights protection in the annual plan on law popularization; provide legal aid and legal services for the elderly; and give full play to the grassroots mediation organizations in older people's rights protection;
- Women's Federation: implement policies to protect the rights and interests of elderly women; organize women to carry out educational programs and various assistance services for the elderly; enrich the spiritual and cultural life of elderly women;

- Bureau of Education: organize various forms educational programs that promote social respects and friendliness to the older people; to organize education professionals to provide services for the elderly;
- Bureau of Public Security: effectively and in a timely way prevent and crack down on illegal activities that harm the rights and interests of the elderly; give lectures which teach older people how to prevent risks and protect themselves; provide the elderly with public security, household registration, transportation, and other services; assure the safety of older people and their property in accordance with the laws and regulations;
- Bureau of Sports: formulate the plan of promoting proper sports among the elderly; publicize and popularize the knowledge and methods of sport for the elderly; provide guidance about scientific exercise for the elderly.

The program is mainly implemented from three dimensions, including organizing community activities, conducting intra-family interventions, and promoting mutual assistance within peer groups. First of all, in terms of community collective activities, it mainly refers to leisure conversations, physical activities, and entertainment activities, which are usually carried out under the organization of the women's federations, community committees, and voluntary organizations according to the mental and physical characteristics of the elderly. Their purpose is to promote the physical and mental health of the elderly and improve their quality of life in late age. There are two prerequisites for the development of community collective activities, namely, love for the elderly services and sincere respect for the elderly. Specific activities include lectures, sports meetings, free legal consultations, and psychological counseling. During the important festivals such as the Spring Festival, Mid-Autumn Festival, and Double Ninth Festival, activities such as joyful art performances would be held in the countryside. These collective activities fully consider the physical conditions of older people: leisure conversations and indoor games are mainly for those aged 75 or above; participants between 65 and 75 years old would be encouraged to have outdoor activities; while for those under 65 years, no special limitations would be applied.

Professionals, including social workers and psychological therapists, would play a key role in these community group activities. These people use professional methods and skills to carry out targeted psychological counseling, family intervention, as well as convey mental health literacies through lectures. As with group activities, themed entertainment, and leisure, the women's federation and community committees would lead older people with similar interests to carry out mutual assistance, policy advocacy, leisure sports, gardening activities, and other activities increasing older people's psychological wellbeing. As for volunteering activities, local public welfare organizations and voluntary service organizations play active roles, which will provide free consultations and farming assistance, and organize poverty alleviation activities for rural older people.

The project also carried out intra-family interventions, and the main forms of intervention can be divided into three types. The first type is to organize intergenerational family interaction parties. During the major traditional festivals such as the Mid-Autumn Festival and the Spring Festival, many migrant workers return to their rural hometowns. With the family as a unit, the women's federation organizes get-togethers of elderly people, their children, daughters-in-law, sons-in-law, or partners to participate in parties, aiming to promote intergenerational exchange and increase family intimacy. The second type is to promote gratitude education activities among the older people's children. Targeting older people's children, the project holds training sessions and group activities, in order to teach these children to be grateful to their parents and share the caregiving responsibilities. At the same time, they also promote regular contacts and communications between the gatekeeper and the children of the elderly participants, and regularly hold "The Most Beautiful Family" selection activities to praise and reward the children who respect and care for elderly parents. Third, the project also actively encourages the elderly to seek happiness and entertainment by themselves.

Finally, the project will conduct seven types of activity-based intervention for older people in the three groups. The first is to promote mutual support within peer groups. The gatekeepers who are responsible for the intervention divide the older people into groups. Each of these groups is comprised of three to four members, and one of the members is selected as the convener to organize and lead various activities. The second is about knowledge transfer. That is, to deliver lectures on the mental health of the elderly, the protection of the rights and interests of the elderly, and to prevent the risk of being deceived in the intervention villages. The third is to establish a regular peer communication mechanism. Under this mechanism, the conveners and gatekeepers invite older people in the risk group and the high-risk group to play cards, sing songs, and participate in leisure conversations every now and then. The fourth is to establish a mechanism of regular visits to older people's home and make records. Gatekeepers and conveners are required to visit at least once a month. The fifth is to form a hobby-based team that allows middle-aged and older people to have cultural activities with local characteristics and to enrich their daily lives. The sixth intervention type is to establish an activity room for the local elderly, which is equipped with chess, playing cards, and other amenities, so that the elderly have the opportunity to gather together. The final type of intervention is to organize various activities in festivals to enhance older people's sense of community and attachment and to reduce their loneliness.

References

Burnette, C., Ramchand, R., & Ayer, L. (2015). Gatekeeper training for suicide prevention: A theoretical model and review of the empirical literature. *Rand Health Quarterly*, *5*(1), 16–30.

Cahn, E., & Rowe, J. (1992). *Time Dollars: The New Currency That Enables Americans to Turn Their Hidden Resource–Time–into Personal Security & Community Renewal*. Boyertown, PA: Emmaus.

Chen, G., & Huang, G. (2017). Time bank's localization, practices, and innovations: A new approach to dealing with the population aging in China (in Chinese). *Journal of Peking University (Social Sciences)*, *54*(6), 111–120.

Collom, E. (2005). Community currency in the United States: The social environments in which it emerges and survives. *Environment and Planning A*, *37*(9), 1565–1587.

Fei, X. (1992). *From the Soil*. Berkeley, CA: University of California Press.

Ginsburg, I. F., & Eng, C. (2009). On-site mental health services for PACE (program of all-inclusive care for the elderly) centers. *Journal of the American Medical Directors Association*, *10*(4), 277–280.

Jiang, Y. (2020, August 19, 2020). Shanghai has established 268 comprehensive services center for the elderly and 187 community-based long-term care home. *Xinmin Evening News*.

Li, M., & Cao, H. (2019). The development of the time banking model and its implications for China's mutual support care for the elderly in the context of population aging (in Chinese). *International Social Science*, *1*, 12–19.

National PACE Association. (2014). *Behavioral Health Operational Resources Toolkit*. Retrieved from https://www.npaonline.org/sites/default/files/PDFs/Intro to NPA Behavioral Health Operational Resources Toolkit.pdf

National PACE Association. (2018). *PACE in the States*. National PACE Association. Unpublished, received by e-mail from Asmaa Albaroudi, Manager of Quality and Policy Initiatives.

Nejati, M., Salamzadeh, Y., & Salamzadeh, A. (2011). Ecological purchase behaviour: insights from a Middle Eastern country. *International Journal of Environment and Sustainable Development*, *10*(4), 417–432.

Valek, L., & Bures, V. (2018). *Time Bank as a Complementary Economic System: Emerging Research and Opportunities: Emerging Research and Opportunities*. Hershey, PA: IGI Global.

6 Locally developed initiatives to contain elderly depression in urbanizing China

6.1 The mutual-support care model

Mutual support between community residents is a long tradition in both rural and urban China. In 2012, China issued the *Law on the Protection of Older People's Rights and Interests*, which explicitly advocates for the establishment of mutual support programs among older people across the country. In the urban sector, various models have been in practice, such as the Time Savings ("时间储蓄") in Beijing, the Old Buddy Program ("老伙伴计划") in Shanghai, the Service Savings ("劳务储蓄") in Tianjin, the Partner Assistance Program ("结对帮扶") in Nanjing, and the Mutual Help Between Silver Hair ("银龄互助") in Guangzhou. According to the evaluation results of Chen and Shi (2015), most of these urban community-based programs were not functioning well and were suffering from low safety, limited transferability, chaotic organizational management, and insufficient credibility.

On the other hand, the mutual-support care model is gaining increased popularity in rural China. According to Wang, Sun, and Xu (2014), faced with the weakening role of family members in supporting the elderly in the process of urbanization, many rural villages have explored new ways of long-term care provision based on the mutual-support principle. Liu (2017) summarized three reasons for the wide application and success of the mutual-support care model in rural China. Firstly, villages and civic organizations can get governmental support when exploring this cost-effective care model. It is apparent that government alone is not able to accommodate the care needs of the fast-increasing rural older population. Thus, encouraging the third sector and other stakeholders to play a more significant role, mainly through government procurement, subsidies, and tax and rent reduction, becomes a preferred approach for local governments. For instance, the major policy documents on elderly care services development by Chinese central government, including *Regulations on the*

DOI: 10.4324/9781003248767-6

Establishment of Elderly Care Service System (2011-2015), *State Council's Opinions on the Enhancement of Elderly Care Industries* (2013), and *The Thirteenth Five-Year Plan on Civil Affairs* (2016), have all explicitly promised more support for rural mutual-support care model.

Secondly, rural older people have relatively lower expectations of care services. Usually, daily instrumental care services that do not require high professional skills, such as cooking, washing, and house cleaning, can easily win their satisfaction. Finally, the principle of mutual support is deeply rooted in Chinese rural society. The informal mutual support network, comprising neighbors, families, and clan members, has always been an indispensable part of Chinese rural people's daily lives, which compensates for the insufficiency of governmental support. In the urbanization process, local and newly introduced civic organizations like social worker associations and elderly associations, together with village committees, further substantiate the role of this informal network. Thus, the development of a mutual-support care model has a solid cultural and organizational foundation in rural China. As a practical and feasible option, the low-cost, widely covered, sustainable, and varied care services provided by the model can offset the influences led by decreasing family size and outmigration of the children's generation in the rural sector.

6.1.1 The case of Four Halls (Si Tang Jian)

As a representative mutual-support care model, the Four Halls model has been developed in the Fengxian District of Shanghai since 2015. As a suburban district, Fengxian held 152,800 older population (60 years and above) in 2015, among which 24,000 people were 80 years or above. At the same time, it had 70,000 households solely comprising older people, and more than 13,000 older people were living alone. As an economically underdeveloped area in suburban Shanghai, Fengxian District's older people are mostly living in rural villages, follow a traditional way of life, and have strong attachment to old houses and land. From September 2015, the district established the first "Four Halls". In this facility, the older people can not only have affordable but good-quality lunches, but also participate in activities such as reading books and newspapers, health lectures, and art performances with local characteristics.

The so-called Four Halls refers to the dining hall for eating, the guest hall for chatting, the school hall for studying, and the discussion hall for social participation. It not only solves the difficulty of preparing meals for rural older people, but also gradually becomes a spiritual and cultural paradise for the elderly. It has created a rural care model that features the self-determination, autonomy, and mutual support of older people.

The development of the Four Halls has enabled many rural older people to get rid of the label of being left behind and to start a new life, that is, to go out of their households and participate in collective activities in the village. The role of older people in developing the facility is impressive: they can decide the location of the facility, negotiate the price of meals, discuss how to carry out group activities, and determine the design of the inner and surrounding environment. Four Halls not only provides basic instrumental care, but also allows the elderly to make choices: "What kind of elderly care services do I want?" and "What I can do for other elderly people?" At present, more than 100 Four Halls have been established across suburban Shanghai, displaying a variety of development forms. For instance, Fengcheng Township uses the Four Halls as a platform to mobilize the elderly to participate in community management, encouraging them to join in environmental protection activities. Qingcun Township adopts a menu-based service delivery model, and various governmental departments provide optional menus, such as medical services and legal consultations, and the elderly in the Four Halls take orders on demand. Nanqiao Township has introduced a volunteer service team comprising children. The team regularly gives singing, dancing, recitation, and music instrumental performances to the elderly in the Four Halls. Children of the team also help by trimming older people's nails, doing massage, and doing cleaning work, to promote intergenerational inclusiveness. Jinhui Township has developed a mediation room model, inviting the elderly in the Four Halls to use their prestige to help the villagers to handle conflicts and disputes.

6.2 The dementia-friendly community model

With the accelerating population aging process, dementia is becoming an increasingly serious public health problem both for China and the world as a whole. According to estimates by the World Health Organization, as of 2017, there are approximately 50 million people with dementia in the world, and more than 10 million of them live in China (Xu, Zhang, Qiu, & Cheng, 2017). By 2030, this number will increase to 82 million, and if the necessary measures are not taken, the number of people living with dementia worldwide will reach 152 million by 2050 (Patterson, 2018). Dementia will significantly increase the economic and care burden of the government, communities, and families, and reduce the quality of life of older people and their caregivers. There are currently about 10 million people with dementia in China. As the city with the highest percentage of older people in the country, Shanghai has more reasons to develop a feasible community service model for people living with dementia.

In 2017, as a professional social organization for dementia, Jian'Ai Charity established a long-term cooperative relationship with the Changshou Road subdistrict government, and took the lead to launch the country's first five-year plan on community services for people living with dementia in Shanghai. At present, this localized practice has gradually formed a complete community solution that includes policy research, industry promotion, resource allocation, professional services, and effectiveness evaluation. It has become a model project in the city's efforts of building a dementia-friendly community service system.

This project is mainly focused on addressing three problems in China's response to dementia: (1) the general public's awareness of dementia is still relatively low, while the misunderstandings caused by traditional concepts and unprofessional services is high; (2) the low willingness of older people and their relatives to see a doctor in the early stages, together with the lack of clinical psychiatric doctors, high misdiagnosis rates, and insufficient public resources such as rehabilitation and community health management; and (3) the lack of top-level design and policy support, as well as the shortage of social services and support networks, and the still increasing long-term care pressures and costs. During the implementation of this project, the organization forms six principles: including (1) "one framework", that is, a dementia-friendly community that integrates medical and healthcare resources; (2) "one system", that is, the dementia evaluation and prevention system; (3) "one mode", namely the Whole Process Management Service Mode; (4) "different stages, different service packages", that is, three older populations are identified, including early-stage healthy population, early-stage risk population, and late-stage disease population, and different services will be provided; (5) "precise services", that is, for different older people the following services will be applied: literacy education, risk screening, early intervention, treatment and rehabilitation, and care support; and (6) "cooperation between stakeholders", that is, the government, social organizations, and enterprises should work together on the problem of dementia care. At the same time, the Jian'Ai Charity also created six subprojects, including: (1) "Memory School", which is titled National Brain Health Education and Promotion Project; (2) "Gas Station for the Brain", which is for brain-health risk early screening and assessment for community-dwelling older people; (3) "Jing Ming Hui", which refers to Body and Brain Activation Center and is for community early intervention for elderly brain health; (4) "Memory Clinic", which is combined with the community health center; (5) "Don't Forget Me", which is a subproject on giving supports to informal caregivers of older people living with dementia; and 6) "Memory Homeland", which is a government-subsidized project for the formal care of people living with dementia.

The implementation of the program comprises five steps. Step 1 is to conduct extensive brain-health science promotion activities. Changshou Road subdistrict has opened a "memory school" in the community through the government's purchase of professional social organization services (the top ten public welfare projects in Shanghai selected by the public welfare application), recruiting and nurturing a group of dementia-friendly people in the community. Through this step of work, cognition and dementia literacy have been largely promoted among volunteers, hospitals, community health centers, companies on long-term care, social organizations, and other caring enterprises and institutions. Moreover, Jian'Ai selects the top ten volunteers for dementia services and the top ten dementia-friendly organizations. The organization also initiated the National Brain Health Education and Promotion Project to eliminate discrimination, improve cognition, and promote health management. In the process, Changshou Road residents and other stakeholders have steadily promoted effective dementia prevention methods, changed misconceptions, eliminated ambiguity, improved cognition, advocated scientific concepts of brain health, and gradually formed a dementia-friendly community.

The second step is to carry out early brain-health screening and demand research. Through cooperation with universities and the teaching hospitals, the Shanghai Jian'Ai Charity Development Center has jointly developed the "Early Dementia Intelligent Screening APP". Relying on an electronic platform called 1+X community network service cloud, the "Gas Station for the Brain" project carries out a series of services in pilot communities, including early screening of symptoms of dementia and compiling brain-health files for people over 55 years. Through taking advantage of the subdistrict's public resources, reforming the referral system of local hospitals, increasing the rate of early consultation and diagnosis of mild cognitive impairment and dementia in the community, the project has created a cognitive health database for older residents.

A specific step taken is to initiate a gas station for brain, which is an early risk screening and assessment project for the elderly's brain health. The project explores the feasibility of community screening, and tries to establish a three-level prevention network through forming strategical cooperation with the teaching hospitals. The mutual referral channel between the hospitals and communities closely connects the pre- and post-diagnosis services. It is worth noting that the function of this channel is strengthened by the empowerment of dementia-friendly ambassadors and dementia-friendly institutions, early diagnosis and risk detection, and the establishment of a community brain-health data cloud platform.

The third step is to promote early intervention mechanisms for brain health. Through the analysis of the basic community data collected in the previous stage, Changshou subdistrict digs deep into local community resources, invites professional agencies to deliver services, design service standards, and improve the service quality of day-care centers for demented older people, and provides regular day care and rehabilitation training for people with mild to moderate cognitive impairment and their family caregivers.

On this basis, Changshou Road subdistrict has established the city's first community center for body–brain activation, which provides professional services to older people with mild cognitive impairment (MCI). MCI contributes to more than 30% of dementia cases and thus is commonly recognized as a significant risk factor for dementia (Breton, Casey, & Arnaoutoglou, 2019). The body–brain activation center provides pre-diagnosis services and treatment and extends services to families, promoting early diagnosis and early intervention in order to reduce the incidence of dementia in the community. The specific practice is to embed the Jingminghui community body–brain activation center into the original day-care center of the community. The upgraded day-care center carries out early intervention services, establishes a service menu and evaluation standards, and introduces a referral mechanism and payment system.

The fourth step is to explore professional care models. This project invited a British healthcare company which has long-term exploration in designing professional dementia care models, integrating resources, and upgrading professional care in institutions. At the same time, the project also established a family support center called "Don't Forget Me", which has become a mutual support platform for dementia family caregivers to interact with each other. This center also empowers family caregivers by providing professional training or respite care services, organizing peer support groups, and facilitating cognitive rehabilitation.

Basically, the missions of the "Don't Forget Me" family support center include: (1) establishing a system of mutual referral between hospitals and communities after diagnosis; (2) enhancing the effectiveness of non-pharmaceutical interventions; (3) providing comprehensive services and professional supports to family caregivers of older people living with moderate to severe dementia; and (4) effectively reducing the family caregiving burden and increasing the quality of life of demented older people through practicing the "people-centered" care model. With the help of social workers, this center forms an accurate match of service demands and supplies; that is, to design services based on the needs of families with demented older people and to ensure the feasibility and professionalism of services through the local support network. At the same time, it pays special attention to human resources training, in order to improve the professional caliber of the service centers in the community.

The final step is to build a dementia-friendly community. To achieve this goal, the project develops a grading and prevention system for dementia, which has been continuously revised and upgraded in real-life management situations. It also improves the informal care support system at the community level and gradually forms a whole process management philosophy. That is, a service model from prevention, treatment, to caregiving. And to make this model work in a desirable context, the project not only initiates the restructuring of the physical environment of the community, but also makes efforts to create a humanistic social environment. Moreover, it stresses the service quality of community agencies and sustainable caregiving by the family members.

References

Breton, A., Casey, D., & Arnaoutoglou, N. A. (2019). Cognitive tests for the detection of mild cognitive impairment (MCI), the prodromal stage of dementia: Meta-analysis of diagnostic accuracy studies. *International Journal of Geriatric Psychiatry*, *34*(2), 233–242.

Chen, Y., & Shi, Y. (2015). Time bank: Origin, problems, and prospects (in Chinese). *Journal of Humanities*, *12*, 111–118.

Liu, N. N. (2017). Mutual support and cooperation: Research on the mutual-support care model in rural China (in Chinese). *Population Studies*, *41*(4), 72–81.

Patterson, C. (2018). *World Alzheimer Report 2018: The State of the Art of Dementia Research: New Frontiers*. London: Alzheimer's Disease International (ADI).

Wang, X., Sun, S., & Xu, Y. (2014). Aging in place services of rural China: SWOT analysis and development strategies (in Chinese). *Hebei Journal*, *34*(2), 94–97.

Xu, J., Zhang, Y., Qiu, C., & Cheng, F. (2017). Global and regional economic costs of dementia: A systematic review. *The Lancet*, *390*(S4), S47.

7 Conclusion

Advocating for urbanization policies that address depression in older population

This research revealed a comprehensive picture of the social determinants for the depression of the Chinese rural older population in the context of urbanization. That is, urbanization can be associated with both positive and negative effects on the depression of the Chinese rural older population at the level of individual life course, household, and community. As a multidimensional social process, urbanization was conceptualized into social identity transformation, household living- arrangement shift, and community environment restructuring according to China's context. Based on the socio-ecological perspective on human development, three quantitative analyses were conducted to examine the dynamics within each level of the influencing factors. Furthermore, three models that are localized from the popular care models in Western countries are introduced, including the Comprehensive Services Center for the Elderly, Time Bank, and the Mental Health Crisis Intervention Program for the Rural Elderly; and the two locally developed initiatives that contain elderly depression in urbanizing China, namely the mutual-support care model and the dementia-friendly community model, are analyzed. The evolution of these models is a reflection of the core principle of China's urbanization policies, namely person-centeredness.

Looking into China's urbanization process is a desirable angle from which to understand China's way of governance. Especially, examining how the country includes maintaining the mental health of an urbanization-affected older population into the goals of its urbanization policies may reveal the fact that China is an "affective state" (Yang, 2013) and the logic of its affection-based governance. An increasing body of literature has been on China's formal policies and informal practices that aim for emotion relaxation and psychological comfort, such as "sending warmth" to the poor at major festivals, mobilizing human and material resources from the urban and rich parts to the remote areas, and the stress of increasing "people's sense of gain" in implementing social policies (Xi, 2015).

DOI: 10.4324/9781003248767-7

Modernization is a core theme of urbanization. China is no exception, and the country shows eagerness to harvest benefits such as economic growth and a modernized national governance system from the process (China National Broadcasting Network, 2013). However, more and more studies have reported the limitations of applying a theoretical framework of modernization defined by Western countries to China. Compared with hot and rigorous discussion on legalization and institutions in establishing a "modern" governance system, little attention has been paid to the affection of people, which actually is deeply embedded in the Chinese political and social texture. Rather than understanding the state as an organization of violence that is formed by rational citizens' power transfer, the Chinese people views the state as a subject that substantially constitutes individuals' affection and morality (Xiang, 2010). Chinese society has long been recognized as a society that balances affection and rationality, and rationality never prevails. This fundamental trait decides that China's governance system should not only be based on rational legislation and institutional design, but affection also plays a significant role. Therefore, while "sending warmth", mobilizing rich areas' resources to the poorer areas, and increasing "people's sense of gain" would be interpreted as the by-products of patriarchism, populism, or centralism according to Western theories, they are recognized as heart-wining projects greatly favored by most Chinese people (He, 2016). That is because these policy practices closely link people and government, and express the care and considerations of one party to the other, which is a reflection of "Ren'ai" proposed by Confucianism. Following this paradigm, it becomes understandable that maintaining the mental health of urbanization-affected older people and caring for their feelings and psychological needs would be considered in China's urbanization policies and practices.

There are several limitations to this research. First, the three quantitative studies are based on the cross-sectional data retrieved from the CHARLS-Baseline. Therefore, it is not able to demonstrate whether the variations on urban identity, household living arrangements, and community environment had causal effects on the depression of the Chinese rural older population. The second limitation is in relation to data availability. Using secondary data, the three quantitative studies were not able to include in analyses some relevant variables that were not available in the datasets. For instance, the individual-level study was only able to focus on a small range of childhood adversity variables. Although the seven variables cover the aspects of childhood life trauma, health and function, and family SES, they can hardly give a full picture of the respondents' adverse childhood experience. This problem also applies to the community-level study, which did not examine or control for some important community-level factors other than the physical and socioeconomic environment, such as crime rate, community cohesion, and the availability of mental health services. Past literature has well documented the significant mental health effects of these factors (Kirmayer, Simpson, & Cargo, 2003; Pirkola, Sund, Sailas, & Wahlbeck, 2009). Also, due to the unavailability of information, the studies were not able to control for micro-level protective factors, such as personal traits, problem-solving skills, peer affiliation, and the adaptation process, which can be essential determinants for one's mental health (Luhmann, Hofmann, Eid, & Lucas, 2012; Mulder, 2014; Sowislo & Orth, 2013).

The third limitation is in relation to the deficiencies in variable coding. In the individual-level quantitative study, some childhood adversities (e.g., childhood physical health conditions) were coded according to the retrospective information reported by the research subjects. This reporting style may add to the inaccuracy of data. Also, when coding the "born at the famine year" variable, the provincial level data on famines were used. This may lead to the imposition of famine experience to individual respondents, although the famines selected were well recognized as the most devastating natural disasters that happened in modern China's history and were supposed to influence the whole population to different degrees in the affected region. With regard to the household-level study, using the frequency of contact with children as the proxy for the received emotional support might not be a good choice. This is because frequency does not necessarily mean quality of relationship and psychological support, and people may have contact with each other just because they want to have a quarrel.

Finally, it is worth noting that the actual effects of urbanization on the depression of the Chinese rural older population may be more complicated than the comprehensive picture outlined in this research. On the one hand, although social identity transformation, household living-arrangement shift, and community environment restructuring are the most significant influencing factors at the individual, household, and community levels, respectively, in China's context, many other factors at each level can also play an important role. At the individual level, for example, past literature has demonstrated that lifestyle, occupation, and consumer behavior are significantly associated with one's mental health (Gong et al., 2012; Marsella, 1998; McMartin, Jacka, & Colman, 2013), while transformations in these aspects go along with the urbanization process. At the household level, apart from living-arrangement shift, Chinese rural families may also experience relocation, denser living space, increased household expenditure, and welfare arrangement change in the urbanization process (Gong et al., 2012; Zhang, 2008). These factors may also impose direct and/or indirect impacts on one's mental wellbeing. At the community level, the increased noise and pollution sources, walkability, neighborhood design, and public services availability have all been demonstrated as significant factors influencing individuals' mental health (Evans, 2003). On the other hand, the influences of urbanization on mental health may lie beyond the individual, household, and community levels. As a macro process with profound impacts, urbanization is also closely associated with the societal/national and global agenda, such as environmental change, poverty, and governance capacity (Grimmond, 2007; Ravallion, Chen, & Sangraula, 2007; Smith, 1996). Due to the availability of research materials, this research involved few macro-level factors.

Despite the limitations, this study makes a contribution to extending the understanding of the relationship between significant events in different life stages, household living arrangements, and community restructuring and depression in the context of urbanization. At the individual level, it streamlines the correlation between childhood life experience and depression in later life by taking into account the moderating role of macro social environment change (i.e., urbanization) happening in-between; at the household level, it looks beyond the previous model of "out-migration of child and remittances from child" and examines the buffering effects of monetary support from all possible family members; and at the community level, it relates community change and individual mental wellbeing through investigating the mediating role of physical and socioeconomic environment factors.

By doing these things, the research presents the following theoretical implications. First, it analyzes the social determinants for the depressive symptoms of the mature and older population in the context of urbanization, which adds to the applicability of the socio-ecological model on human development outcomes. As a comprehensive framework comprising microsystem, mesosystem, macrosystem, exosystem, and chronosystem, the socio-ecological framework is in line with the multidimensionality of urbanization. By putting the research within the context of urbanization, the influencing factors of mental health in various systems can be examined in a structured way. Second, by conceptualizing urbanization within a specific country's context, this research provides strong empirical support to the socio-ecological framework. Contextualization is an inherent requirement of the socio-ecological model. Since social texture in different countries or cultures may vary, application of the framework will have quite a weak foundation if social conditions and ecology are not defined. Through defining China's urbanization as social identity transformation at the individual level, living-arrangement shift at the household level, and community environment restructuring at the community level, this research provides support to the framework by generating relevant empirical evidence based on a national population.

At the same time, this research can also present significant policy implications not only for China, but also for other developing countries. With the ongoing trends of population aging and urbanization worldwide, especially in low- and middle-income countries, increased attention has been paid to the intertwining of these two major demographic transitions (Beard & Petitot, 2010). This has evolved into a public concern as how to shape a process of urbanization that facilitates better human development outcomes in later life. With a comprehensive picture being revealed, the related policy initiatives can be made accordingly.

This research proposes that the public sector shall make "person-centeredness" its core principle in shaping an urbanization that is good for the mental wellbeing of the aging population. At the individual level, special attention should be paid to people with inferior prescribed socioeconomic status, such as low family background and childhood health. From a life-course perspective, the World Health Organization and Calouste Gulbenkian Foundation (2014) has proposed that policy interventions that give every child the best possible start in life will generate the greatest mental health benefits all through one's lifetime. Therefore, socially inclusive policies should be introduced within the urbanization context to avoid cumulative disadvantage.

At the household level, policy priority should be given to the mature and older adults whose children have migrated. The absence of children in a household or nearby cannot be replaced for mature and older adults, and their mental health loss resulting from the out-migration of children cannot be compensated for by household income, monetary support from family members, and non-face-to-face contact with children. Therefore, on the one hand, supportive services for the mental wellbeing of left-behind mature and older people should be established, ensuring that they have sufficient resources to buffer the stressors led by the out-migration of children; while on the other hand, the country-level urbanization strategy should be adjusted, that is, by upgrading the rural economy to accommodate local youth labors and thus avoid spatial dispersion of family members.

At the community level, China has, since the mid-1980s, adopted a "community building" strategy nationwide to build community capacity by expanding community-based services. However, rural communities were largely ignored in this policy initiative (Shen, 2014). Taking the opportunity of urbanization, the Chinese rural community is supposed to build itself into an aging-friendly community that includes not only physical environment construction, such as infrastructure and amenity facilities, but also socio-economic environment upgrading, such as the enhancement of local economic structure, the establishment of income protection and other welfare arrangements, and the revival of civil society featuring mutual help as well as self-expression.

This research outlines the associations of urbanization with the depression of the Chinese rural older population, focusing on social identity, living arrangements, and community environment at the individual, household, and community levels, respectively, as well as the country's explorations of models of caring for older people's mental health. This leaves room for future research to investigate. First, future study should examine other factors at each level, such as lifestyle, relocation, living-space change, and neighborhood design. Second, with the increased availability of longitudinal data, more attention should be on the causal relationship between the various urbanization-related factors and the mental health of mature and older adults. Third, since the effects of social determinants of mental health may vary for different people, future study should pay more attention to how affected people cope with stressors and how personal traits are associated with the coping results.

References

Beard, J. R., & Petitot, C. (2010). Ageing and urbanization: Can cities be designed to foster active ageing. *Public Health Reviews*, *32*(2), 427–450.

China National Broadcasting Network. (2013). The troika of Premier Li Keqiang's economic ideology: Employment, urbanization, and reformation. Retrieved from http://finance.cnr.cn/gundong/201311/t20131107_514060138.shtml

Evans, G. (2003). The built environment and mental health. *Journal of Urban Health*, *80*(4), 536–555. doi:10.1093/jurban/jtg063

Gong, P., Liang, S., Carlton, E. J., Jiang, Q., Wu, J., Wang, L., & Remais, J. V. (2012). Urbanisation and health in China. *The Lancet*, *379*(9818), 843–852. doi:10.1016/S0140-6736(11)61878-3

Grimmond, S. (2007). Urbanization and global environmental change: Local effects of urban warming. *The Geographical Journal*, *173*(1), 83–88. doi:10.1111/j.1475-4959.2007.232_3.x

He, X. (2016). Affection-based governance: An important dimension of governance in the era of new media (in Chinese). *Exploration and Contention*, 2016(11), 40–42.

Kirmayer, L., Simpson, C., & Cargo, M. (2003). Healing traditions: Culture, community and mental health promotion with Canadian Aboriginal peoples. *Australasian Psychiatry*, *11*(s1), S15–S23. doi:10.1046/j.1038-5282.2003.02010.x

Luhmann, M., Hofmann, W., Eid, M., & Lucas, R. E. (2012). Subjective well-being and adaptation to life events: A meta-analysis. *Journal of Personality and Social Psychology*, *102*(3), 592. doi:10.1037/a0025948

Marsella, A. J. (1998). Urbanization, mental health, and social deviancy: A review of issues and research. *American Psychologist*, *53*(6), 624. doi:10.1037/0003-066X.53.6.624

McMartin, S. E., Jacka, F. N., & Colman, I. (2013). The association between fruit and vegetable consumption and mental health disorders: Evidence from five waves of a national survey of Canadians. *Preventive Medicine, 56*(3), 225–230. doi:10.1037/a0025948

Mulder, R. T. (2014). Personality pathology and treatment outcome in major depression: A review. *American Journal of Psychiatry, 159*(3), 359–371. doi:10.1176/appi.ajp.159.3.359

Pirkola, S., Sund, R., Sailas, E., & Wahlbeck, K. (2009). Community mental-health services and suicide rate in Finland: A nationwide small-area analysis. *The Lancet, 373*(9658), 147–153. doi:10.1016/S0140- 6736(08)61848-6

Ravallion, M., Chen, S., & Sangraula, P. (2007). New evidence on the urbanization of global poverty. *Population and Development Review, 33*(4), 667–701. doi:10.1111/j.1728-4457.2007.00193.x

Shen, Y. (2014). Community building and mental health in mid-life and older life: Evidence from China. *Social Science & Medicine, 107*, 209–216. doi:10.1016/j.socscimed.2013.12.023

Smith, D. A. (1996). Third World cities in global perspective: The political economy of uneven urbanization. Routledge, New York, USA.

Sowislo, J. F., & Orth, U. (2013). Does low self-esteem predict depression and anxiety? A meta-analysis of longitudinal studies. *Psychological Bulletin, 139*(1), 213. doi:10.1037/a0028931

World Health Organization, & Calouste Gulbenkian Foundation. (2014). *Social Determinants of Mental Health.* Retrieved from Geneva: WHO.

Xi, J. (2015). Make people have more sense of gain from the reform (in Chinese). Retrieved from http://www.xinhuanet.com/politics/2015-02/27/c_1114458700.htm

Xiang, B. (2010). Ordinary people's theory of the "state" (in Chinese). *Open Times,* 2010(10), 117–132.

Yang, J. (2013). Song wennuan,'sending warmth': Unemployment, new urban poverty, and the affective state in China. *Ethnography, 14*(1), 104–125.

Zhang, L. (2008). Conceptualizing China's urbanization under reforms. *Habitat International, 32*(4), 452–470. doi:10.1016/j.habitatint.2008.01.001

9 781032 164854